COSMOPOLIS

YESTERDAY'S CITIES OF THE FUTURE

1.   A city in the clouds: The Woolworth Building (1913), at the time the world's tallest building, led the way as Manhattan reached for the sky and the Cosmopolis of tomorrow.

COSMOPOLIS

YESTERDAY'S CITIES OF THE FUTURE

David Mansfield

HOWARD MANSFIELD

CENTER
FOR URBAN
POLICY RESEARCH

Published by the Center for Urban Policy Research
Building 4051—Kilmer Campus
New Brunswick, New Jersey 08903
All rights reserved
Printed in the United States of America

Library of Congress Cataloging-in-Publication Data

Mansfield, Howard.
    Cosmopolis.

    Includes bibliographical references.
    1. Metropolitan areas. I. Title.
HT330.M34   1990   307.76′4   89-25159
ISBN 0-88285-131-4

The author has made extensive efforts to contact and credit copyright holders of the illustrations reprinted in this book. If copyright proprietorship can be established for any illustration not specifically attributed in the "Credits" section of this book, please contact The Center for Urban Policy Research, Box 489, Piscataway, New Jersey.

Book design by Howard Mansfield

The author gratefully acknowledges Mary Picarella for her invaluable assistance in the production of this book.

To My Parents

Who Knew The Future
When It Was New

2.   *The hand of the creator, in this case Le Corbusier's, looming over his own scale model of the Plan Voisin, points the way to the future.*

CONTENTS

Part I

A GREAT BIG BEAUTIFUL TOMORROW

I remember a show from the 1964–65 World's Fair. The marionettes danced on the stage. "Oh—it's—a—great—big—beautiful—tomorrow," they sang, making stilted marionette motions by tilting their heads to mark every word: "a—great—big—beautiful—tomorrow."

Millions saw that show, and I think of it whenever I read of a new scheme for the future. A family of life-sized marionettes starts out in a turn-of-the-century house and many scenes later ends up in the future. The stage revolves, and with each scene the appliances get newer as the marionettes gracefully age. The wood-burning stove becomes the gas range, electric range, microwave oven. And in the last scene—the great big beautiful tomorrow—there were the space-age shapes of appliances, the magic of the future, so close it made you want to reach up and touch the things on stage. The message was clear: Better things—through consumption—were on the way. Progress was sketched into infinity.

We would leapfrog into the future invention by invention, toaster by blender, appliance by appliance, until at last, all our devices in order, we would arrive at a utopia somewhere the other side of the checkout counter.

Each invention has promised so much. One example, of the hundreds that could be offered, is glass. The mountains of glass we now see around us in cities were once the herald of a new age. At the end of World War I, one architect wrote: "It is not the crazy caprice of a poet that glass will bring a new culture. It is a fact." German architects wrote fervently about the new material. Bruno Taut proposed entire cities of glass. "Hurray for the transparent, the clear!" he wrote in 1919. "Hurray for purity!

3.   "The unformulated, yet gleaming metropolis" portrayed by Hugh Ferriss in 1925. " 'The lure of the city' is the romantic way of phrasing it: imagination sketches the rural youth who is ever arising to his dreams of 'the big city,' " wrote Ferriss.

1

Hurray for crystal! Hurray and again hurray for the fluid, the graceful, the angular, the sparkling, the flashing, the light—hurray for everlasting architecture."

In the end, glass gave us the box for corporate culture—the mundane, the workaday, the nine-to-five face of our downtowns. Similar stories can be told of many of our inventions. (One has only to think of how we were introduced to atomic energy. By 1980, power would be "free like the unmetered air," predicted Dr. John Van Neumann of the Atomic Energy Commission.)

The city, too, has been treated as an invention. Over the last one hundred years a succession of architects, planners, and a stenographer-turned-visionary (Ebenezer Howard) have proposed reordering things, each promising that his was the magic geometry, which like the tumblers on a lock, would open the way to the good life. "Well planned towns will foster well planned lives." That was the reformers' credo.

The spirit of earnest invention and born-again faith in new materials runs through so many of the plans to change the city. The world would be made anew. And at last—at long last—mankind would stand tall and free. The world's cities, wrote the great modern architect Le Corbusier, "could become . . . irresistible forces stimulating collective enthusiasm, collective action, and general joy and pride, and in consequence individual happiness everywhere. . . . The modern world would begin to emerge from behind its labor-blackened face and hands, and would beam around, powerful, happy, believing. . . ."

And what would the "modern world" behold, once it rinsed off its "labor-blackened face"? A world so fantastic it was not even possible until the last years of the nineteenth century; proud cities of towers. Rows of towers in green parks, if it were to be Le Corbusier's world. Rows of towers with a rushing city at the base, if it were to be a metropolis like those envisioned by Francisco Mujica, Hugh Ferriss, and others.

IF there is one invention that embodies the city of the future, it is the skyscraper. It was looked upon as the *answer* to congestion downtown and out in the countryside as a way to bring people closer to nature. All this sounds backward today, but in its infancy the skyscraper was—what else?—but the herald of a new age.

One can catch the excitement that these towers brought forth in the 1908 edition of *King's Views of New York*. "The cosmopolis of the future," it says under a drawing of the world to come, "when the wonder of 1908—the Singer Building, 612 feet high with offices on the 41st floor—will be far outdone, and the 1,000-foot structure realized." Progress was measurable: 612 feet. It was an era when city guides boasted of buildings by adding up the tons of concrete poured and the miles of wiring used. ("If all the wiring were unraveled it would stretch. . . .")

King's Views proudly notes the 150,000 cubic feet of stone used in the Singer Building and its 11 acres of office space all under one roof. (The Singer Building was demolished in 1967.)

Not everyone sounded the chamber of commerce sirens. Henry James, returning to New York City in 1907 after years in Europe, was saddened by the new skyline. Many argued for the abolition of the skyscraper, among them Henry Ford, Thomas Edison, and the editor of the *Journal of the American Institute of Architects*. The debate is captured in this poem:

```
           THE
          S K Y-
       SCRAPER
       T  A  L  L
       I  S        A
       WONDER
       T O   A L L
       A   THING
       TOADMIRE
       B E Y O N D
       QUESTION
```

Butoh!downbelowwherepedestriansgo
itcertainlyaddstocongestion

Among the architects, there were objections sensible and misguided. Thomas Hastings, one of the architects of the New York Public Library, argued in the *New York Tribune* of December 30, 1894, that a steel skeleton would soon rust and inspection would be needed. His partner, John Merzen Carrere, suggested a tax on all buildings above eight stories. George Post, himself an early exponent of the form, believed that towers would stop being built when they started crowding each other out, blocking the sunlight and thus making the lower floors unrentable.

One critic, Major Henry Curran, asked the central question. In a 1927 speech, he said: "Is it good sense not to have a dollar for any other city need, to pour it all into more traffic facilities to take care of a coagulated bunch of skyscrapers? Is that sense? Is that city planning? . . . That is where we are headed."

The skyscraper fever was on the land in the 1920s, and there were many who were convinced that it was the shape of things to come. Where others saw "a coagulated bunch" of towers, Francisco Mujica saw the "climax of constancy and order." Mujica, an architect and Mexican archaeologist, wrote a spirited defense of the tall building and a hymn to its future in his 1929 book, *History of the Skyscraper*.

"How difficult it would be for a New Yorker who had been absent for 40 years to find any feature of the old city panorama which has disappeared under the most formidable construction force ever recorded," Mujica wrote. "Buildings which at that time were considered dominating seem to be crushed by the

Babylonic masses of the city." Up to this point, it sounds as if he were warming up for a lamentation, but Mujica continues: "This represents the highest efforts of man, the greatest achievements of architecture in our century, and the climax of constancy and order, which by the coordinating efforts of poor pygmies has made it possible to build the most stupendous city on earth."

Far from causing congestion, the skyscraper, like every good invention, was a time saver. In his defense of the skyscraper, Mujica quotes from Harvey Wiley Corbett, an influential architect who advocated separating pedestrians on a level over traffic, a feature that became a constant in the skyscraper utopias.

The skyscraper made business more efficient, Corbett argued: "The business area is condensed and time is saved. The skyscraper is one of the modern inventions—a steel speed machine. . . ." In contrast, Corbett offers the example of London, a city at that time of a four-story average, with businesses so scattered about that it was difficult to make three appointments in a day, he said; but the skyscraper, keeping workers off the streets, was "an actual relief of street congestion."

The ideal city of the future, for Corbett and others, would contain entire communities in one building. The base of the tower would be for business. At the tower's first setback, there would be an upper sidewalk "with promenades and terraces in fresh air and sunshine," residences, and stores. The center of the building would have theaters, gyms, and swimming pools.

"When a man left his office, he could take an elevator home," wrote Corbett. "The most congested traffic would be reduced and people could get the full benefit of the light and air available at the top of our cities."

While this may sound confining—like living on a cruise ship that has run aground at 52nd Street—to Corbett it passed that key test of a utopia: It was just what we *needed*. "The tall building, like other honest architectural forms, is the result of fundamental human needs." (How had we lived so long, for millennia, so close to the ground?)

People living outside the city would also have their "needs" met. Industrial designer Norman Bel Geddes proposed replacing Main Street with a skyscraper. In his 1932 book, *Horizons*, he wrote:

"The public at large thinks of skyscraper architecture as applying only to large cities. There are many arguments for its application to the small town. All the merchants in a town of five thousand persons will some day pool their interests. Instead of putting up numerous little three-story and four-story buildings of their own, they will build *one* tower-type building in the center of the town. This tower will not need to be very high, yet it will make life much easier for the whole community. Mrs. Jones will find it more convenient for her shopping, especially in rainy, hot or cold weather. In rainy weather she will be dry from the time she enters the building until she completes her errands. In hot

4.   King's Views of New York (1908) presented this "dream" of the future: "The cosmopolis of the future. A weird thought of the frenzied heart of the world in later times, incessantly crowding the possibilities of aerial and inter-terrestrial construction, when the wonders of 1908—the Singer Building, 612 feet high—will be far outdone, and the 1,000-foot structure realized; now nearly a million people do business here each day; by 1930 it is estimated the number will be doubled, necessitating tiers of sidewalks, with elevated lines and new creations to create subway and surface cars, with bridges between the structural heights. Airships, too may connect us with all the world. What will posterity develop?"

5

weather, the building will be cooled by conditioned air, and in cold weather, heated. She will not be going from one draft temperature to another and slipping on icy pavements. The doctor, the movie and the butcher will all be under one roof, along with the commercial and governmental activities of the town, including the theatre and the mayor's office."

Lay this tower on its side and Bel Geddes has anticipated by thirty years the shopping mall. (In the 1960s, the idea of putting entire communities in one building became something of an architectural rage. "Megastructures" were drawn that dwarfed the island of Manhattan.)

When Mrs. Jones arrived home from shopping in the "our town" tower, she might return to another tower. In many schemes, the tower was seen as a preserver of open space: The skyscraper was not only a time-saving invention, it was a space-saving invention. Le Corbusier had proposed such towers in the green in his Plan Voisin for Paris (1925) and his Ville Radieuse plan (1935). Frank Lloyd Wright and others had worked variations on this idea as a way to update the garden city.

Raymond Hood, one of the architects of New York City's Rockefeller Center, proposed a tower for the countryside in Dobbs Ferry, New York. He offered a classic explanation of his 1932 plan: "Why not make a tower? It fits everybody. The average family of city dwellers dislikes the coal bill, the repair bill, taxes and the countless expenses of running a detached house. He does like open country, trees, lakes, light and air. In a tower he

has it all. Why pull up all those beautiful trees [and] cut up the countryside to form new real estate developments. . . . The city man lives outside the city because he likes the country. Why not give him the country as it is? He can have his house in the tower . . . and the country at his very door, wild and unspoiled." In short, we can have it all. We can be Henry David Thoreau on the twentieth floor.

Not only would the skyscraper bring the city to the country, it would do the reverse: Towers would rise, scruffy tenements would be leveled, and green space, like some inrushing sea, would fill the city. This was Le Corbusier's vision in his many city plans. The tall towers would create enough income, he believed, so that the rest of the space could be left open. This has been one of the more influential ideas in the twentieth century. Almost every city in the world has some fragment of the "Radiant City." It was a seductive vision: a city free of the squalor that reformers had been targeting since Dickens's time; free of the crowded lanes of airless tenements where the "other half" lived.

Raymond Hood showed the influence of the idea in his 1927 plan for a "City of Towers": "The city would throw off its outworn street plan. There would be no cumbersome overhead or underground streets, darkened alleys, fouled air or congested traffic lanes. Eventually there would be no streets. The city would be a park dotted with buildings in which the traffic could go straight in any direction."

5. and 6. The construction of the Singer Tower, the world's tallest building in 1908, was taken as a yardstick of progress. On the facing page, the Singer Tower is compared to the world's tallest structures. On the cover of Scientific American, *June 29, 1907, its height is compared to Victoria Falls and Niagara Falls.*

7. (Overleaf) Francisco Mujica's version of "The City of the Future: Hundred-Story City in Neo-American Style." This drawing from History of the Skyscraper *(1929) shows the main street with a central aerodrome at the end.*

And Norman Bel Geddes argued that if the Empire State Building filled the whole block instead of "merely" a quarter of the block, all those who worked in the surrounding half-dozen blocks could work in this one mega-Empire State Building. "It would release these half-dozen blocks for use as parks."

Of course, the mathematics of real estate development work against this view, and it is hard to believe that such men of the world as Le Corbusier and Bel Geddes did not know this. Build a hundred-story building and you have created land values for more hundred-story buildings, not swing sets and duck ponds.

So the skyscraper was seen as fulfilling contradictory missions. We would have cities of "Babylonic masses," undreamed of wonders with acres of offices under one spire, but we would also have cities with expanses of parks and a countryside preserved close by, cows grazing in the shadow of residential towers. It all depended on who was drawing the plans. Frequently, these two cities were seen existing together.

In his peroration to *History of the Skyscraper,* Mujica envisioned a future both of one-hundred-story buildings ranged like mountains and residential areas of skyscrapers in Eden.

"The city of the future will consist of rhythmic masses of platforms, towers and pyramids making the blue dome of the sky appear framed in gigantic rectilinear outlines. . . ."

But also: "Le Corbusier's plans of residential skyscrapers will be the cradle of tomorrow's strong race, formed under the caress of the sun and in the perfume of flowers."

Mujica was intoxicated with the skyscraper city, and he exhorts us to work for its perfection. "There is still a long way to go, but the vision which is the goal of the American cities can be perceived faintly on the horizon as something great and fine."

The problem of skyscraper design had been solved, he wrote. "Now remains the other part: solving the architectural problem of the city that is about to be created, that is in its formative stage, the vertical city, that will bring about a maximum of economy in this century of speed, and at the same time offer the best possible hygienic conditions."

This great city would come to us, Mujica believed, if we would not "check its progress." (Here he was speaking particularly to those who wanted to abolish the skyscraper.) He invokes the vision of Manhattan as the sign of the promised land to come:

"Let us meet the future halfway, be modern—without breaking with the past—let us be practical, yet setting aside a few moments each day for dreaming . . . and thus work for the development of the modern city, giving it fully the mechanical and practical stamp of our century, yet not forgetting in our planning that each part of this gigantic human machine has a heart capable of soaring high and loving. . . .

"It has been often said that New York has no soul.

"The soul of Manhattan is a new, but a great soul!

"See it at nightfall when the moon sheds her silver light on its rectilinear masses, when thousands of lights scintillate in numberless windowpanes and the waters of the bay, in restless waves, lap against its shores voluptuously, while boats carry messages of the hopes of men. . . .

"At such moments the soul of Manhattan seems to emerge from the very depths of this fantastic conglomeration of enormous masses and, exhorting the city with a caress, cry: *Forwards!*"

THESE celebrations of the glories of the metropolis reached an apotheosis in the drawings of Hugh Ferriss. His dark, atmospheric renderings of skyscrapers were a hallmark of the 1920s.

8.   *"A City of Needles," Hugh Ferriss's rendering of a 1924 proposal by architect Raymond Hood. These 1,000-foot to 1,400-foot skyscrapers are placed over the intersections of highways that crisscross the city. "It would appear, indeed, that such structures would have unusual values as to exposure, light and air," wrote Ferriss; "but probably the greatest virtue of this proposal lies in the implied simplification of transportation. The vertical transportation is, in these narrow towers, visibly centralized, and the entire ground level, throughout the city, is made available for horizontal traffic."*

Using charcoal or carbon pencil, Ferriss drew heroic views of skyscrapers, emphasizing their soaring mass with dramatic lighting and brooding skies. He did not draw an exact photolike image, but rather tried to capture "the emotional tone and particular mood of the building."

Ferriss was called on by the leading architects of the day, including Raymond Hood and Harvey Wiley Corbett, to render

9. Ferriss: "Night in the Science Zone. Buildings like Crystals."

their buildings, and he worked with them on exhibits depicting the city of the future. The Ferriss look quickly came to be what the public expected of the future city: hanging gardens on penthouses, apartment towers on bridges, different levels of pedestrian and automotive traffic, and cliffs of buildings disappearing into the sky. His stylized cities were copied in advertising, science fiction illustrations, and the movies. Ferriss used many of the drawings in his 1929 book, *The Metropolis of Tomorrow.*

Here again is the romantic description of the city. Ferriss opens his book by describing the city emerging from an early morning fog. On a terrace "some visitor from another land or another time" looks out over the clouds. "What apocalypse is about to be revealed? . . . Off in the mist, a single lofty highlight of gold appears: the earliest beam is upon the tip of the Metropolitan tower. . . ." And here again is the discussion of the burgeoning size of skyscrapers. In the 1920s, Manhattan boomed, reaching for the sky as never before. New York had changed more in three years, one observer said, than it had changed in the last twenty.

Ferriss rode that boom and, with the characteristic optimism of the era, believed that the skyscraper would liberate us. In a 1925 interview in the *New York Evening Post,* he said:

"In the future when the evolution of the city is accomplished, the people of New York will actually live in the sky. There will be avenues of aerial gardens and sky golf courses. Instead of going to the country, people will go 'up' for country air. Towering terraced buildings of the residential zone will give the children a chance to play out of doors. Everybody in the city will spend more time in the open. There will be aerial hangars and airplanes will be as common as flivvers."

But in the "imaginary metropolis" he presents in his book, this almost giddy view from the heights disappears. The center of his future city is in the shape of two stars: a smaller star set within a larger one. At the center is a park two miles in diameter. Anchoring three corners of the largest star are 1,000-foot towers that announce the major zones: business, science, and art. Avenues radiate out from these tall towers, lined with lesser buildings and parks. No residences, no hospitals, no schools are in view.

This is the description of the Science Zone:

> Buildings like crystal
> Walls of translucent glass
> Sheer glass blocks sheathing a steel grill
> No Gothic branches:
>   No acanthus leaf:
>   no recollections of the plant world

A mineral kingdom
Gleaming stalagmites
Forms as cold as ice
Mathematics
Night in the Science Zone.

The metropolis of tomorrow is hardly a place you want to even visit. The same can be said of Mujica's mountains of skyscrapers or Le Corbusier's or Hood's plans. Whether the towers are massed in a "coagulated bunch," dispersed in greenery, or arranged in star patterns, what all these cities share in common is that they are big. It is perhaps too bald a fact to need stating, but the world of tomorrow, as envisioned in the 1920s and 1930s, would be a big place where men did big deeds. These cities are stage sets for heroic acts. Looking down from the heights (these plans are always drawn from a God's-eye view), it is difficult to imagine oneself setting out among the towers with a list of errands in hand. Where in the Business Zone would you find a bakery? (Where at all in this city would there be the smell of fresh bread?) What restaurant or bar would stay open late in the Science Zone?

For all the views of rushing traffic and towers marching into the distance, Ferriss's metropolis is an oddly static place. It is the stasis of utopias. "All ideal models have the same life-arresting, if not denying, property," wrote Lewis Mumford in one of his many meditations on utopia. When Plato designed his Republic, the pattern was set and all change banished, notes Mumford. So it has been with every utopia. "Compared with even the simplest manifestations of spontaneous life within the teeming environment of nature, every utopia is, almost by definition, a sterile desert, unfit for human occupation," writes Mumford.

BUT that's not how the story ends. The story begins in paradise and ends in utopia. Through prosperity and hard times, the promise of utopia did not diminish. At its publication in 1929, Ferriss's book, *The Metropolis of Tomorrow,* was enthusiastically received. One reviewer said Ferriss was "a poet among architects, an artist who can translate in terms of steel, the soaring aspirations of man." The Great Crash that same year brought the skyscraper boom to an end, but, if anything, the Depression intensified the longing for a better tomorrow. In the Depression, anyone who came along with a better idea could audition to be a prophet.

If there was one future people voted for, it was the "Futurama" at the 1939 World's Fair. More than five million people saw that show, at times having to wait in lines that stretched for a mile. In the General Motors exhibit, the inventive Norman Bel Geddes had worked up a sight for Depression-weary eyes: the world of 1960.

10.   *The Business Center. "The tower itself rises directly over the intersection of two of the master highways, to the height of 1,200 feet. There are eight flanking towers, half this height, which, with their connecting wings, enclose four city blocks. The center extends, however, over eight adjoining blocks, where its supplementary parts rise to a height of 12 stories," wrote Ferriss.*

Each person sat in an armchair that moved along a conveyor, providing a 16-minute flight over the world of tomorrow. Sitting down, the first thing the time traveler heard, from a speaker in the back of the chair, was: "Strange? Fantastic? Unbelievable? Remember, this is the world of 1960."

Then below, as if seen from a low-flying plane, the wonders unfolded. It was a landscape crossed by high-speed highways on which teardrop-shaped cars sped along at 100 miles per hour, past experimental farms and orchards (where each tree was under its own glass sphere) and headed toward the city. There were tall curving towers of glass and blocks of greenery. About one-third of the city was parkland. At the base of the towers, the highways met in massive intersections, in places more than twenty lanes wide. (This future was, after all, sponsored by General Motors.) No pedestrians were in sight.

In creating the Futurama, Bel Geddes had used actual American cities—St. Louis, Missouri; Council Bluffs, Iowa; Reading, Pennsylvania; New Bedford, and Concord, Massachusetts; Rutland, Vermont; Omaha, Nebraska; and Colorado Springs, Colorado—and projected them twenty years ahead. The ideas

11.   "Strange? Fantastic? Unbelievable? Remember, this is the world of 1960." With those words, visitors to the Futurama sat back in their chairs and saw the wonderworld of 1960: lanes and lanes of high-speed traffic, tall glass towers, experimental farms, huge hydropower projects, modern campuses, and amusement parks.

were once again mostly from Le Corbusier, towers in the green and rushing automotive traffic. Bel Geddes also borrowed heavily from Frank Lloyd Wright's Broadacre City plan, which had been exhibited a few years earlier at Rockefeller Center.

E. B. White reported on his visit to the fair in *Harper's* magazine. "A ride on the Futurama of General Motors induces approximately the same emotional response as a trip through the Cathedral of St. John the Divine," he wrote. "When night falls in the General Motors exhibit and you lean back in the cushioned chair (yourself in motion and the world so still) and hear (from the depths of the chair) the soft electric assurance of a better life—the life which rests on wheels alone—there is a strong, sweet poison which infects the blood. I didn't want to wake up. I liked 1960 in purple light, going a hundred miles an hour around impossible turns ever onward toward the certified cities of the flawless future." But White went on to record his doubts when he saw the orchard trees under glass globes.

Near the end of the excursion, the chairs passed close by one intersection from the city of 1960, and the travelers heard: "In a moment we will arrive on this very street intersection—to become part of this self-same scene in the World of Tomorrow—in the wonder world of 1960—1939 is twenty years ago! *All eyes to the future!*" Sure enough, there they were. Having flown over this fantastic world of 1960, visitors now stood at a full-size street corner—in the *future!*

One hates to be a killjoy, but it was already in 1939, an old future. The intersection was modeled on Harvey Wiley Corbett's 1927 proposal: pedestrians above and traffic below. Some cold-water critics did note that strangely the streets of 1960 were filled with "General Motors trucks and cars, definitely of 1939 vintage."

The Futurama was one of many future visions at the 1939 World's Fair and by far the most popular. There was a "Town of Tomorrow," a "Rocketport of the Future," a "Dairy World of Tomorrow," a "Soda Fountain of the Future," and even, going it all one better, "The World of the Day After Tomorrow." In the Perisphere, which along with the Trylon was the Fair's symbol, there was "Democracity." Centron was its hub, with a single one-hundred-story glass skyscraper and streets radiating out toward the greenbelt and some seventy satellite towns. Visitors looked down on this world from a rotating balcony and saw a day pass below. The lighting reproduced a 24-hour day in five and a half minutes. As dusk fell and the stars came out, "a thousand-voice chorus came from the heavens, and from equidistant points on the horizon came marchers, representing various groups in society," wrote Francis E. Tyng in *Making a World's Fair*. "The marchers increased in size, then vanished beyond drifting clouds. A blaze of polarized light was the climax."

There was no question who was leading the marchers on, who would lead the country out of hard times into the wonders of

1960: the engineer, the industrial designer. Each utopia is set in motion by some hand that usually expects to be the philosopher-king of that newborn realm. In many plans, particularly the sky-scraper utopias of the 1920s, the question of who would lead was left vague. (Very likely those who had amassed the capital to build so high.) Still, in the 1930s, it was clear. Bel Geddes portrayed good design as a life-and-death matter. The industrial designer, he wrote, "is a parallel to the lawyer who *wins* his case and the surgeon who *saves* a life. There is no middle ground." We would plan our way out of the Depression. After all, as Bel Geddes wrote, "Well planned communities will foster well planned lives."

The prophets of the future in the 1920s and earlier sound like car dealers and door-to-door salesmen. They are pitching us the future, delivering a chamber of commerce pep talk; but in the 1930s, there was a totalitarian ring to the rhetoric. We lead—you follow. What each era's prophets have in common is a belief in efficiency as the highest ideal. The 1936 film, *Things to Come,* captures this well. The film is based on an H. G. Wells story. It is Christmas 1940 in "Everytown." War breaks out and rages for the next thirty years. The world is in disarray, reduced to rubble and tribelike fiefdoms, when a slender fellow dressed in black arrives by air. He represents the new order, and he is prone to long-winded speeches (which will evidently be a staple of the new order). While introducing himself, he says repeatedly, "I am the law and sanity," and also that he does not approve of independent sovereign states. He explains: "We who are all that's left of the old engineers and mechanics, we have placed our-selves to salvage the world. . . . We have ideas in common. The brotherhood of efficiency, the last trustees of civilization."

Bel Geddes elaborated on the ideas behind the Futurama show in a book published the following year, *Magic Motorways* (1940). The book is a call for a national highway system run-ning straight and true across the continent. Old roads follow cat-tle paths, Bel Geddes said, and were hopelessly snarled down-town. His plan would have the motorways run near cities but never through them. Comparatively little is said about city design in the book.

He takes the reader on a trip across the country on the new motorways, roads that "never veer." The driver surrenders con-trol of his car to an automatic guidance system and whisks along at 100 miles per hour. The northern-most motorway would start fifty miles outside Boston and head through upstate New York. "It crosses Niagara above the falls; without swerving, it hurries through the province of Ontario, crosses Lake St. Clair north of Detroit . . . and makes straight for Lake Michigan. At this point the lake is fifty miles wide. Never mind. There is no let down on the motorway. It shoots directly across the lake on a long bridge." Having subdued the Great Lakes, the motorway heads straight toward the Rockies.

The statement "never mind" encapsulates the flip side of progress. Throughout the postwar years, "never mind" has been the implied refrain every time a highway tore through a neighborhood or a redwood forest was cut down. Never mind. It is the implied refrain hiding behind "the world of 1960." Level one-third of downtown for parks? Trees under separate glass spheres? Never mind. If we were naming utopias in the classical tradition, we could call the Futurama the Land of Never Mind.

12.   *The marchers appear on the horizon in the finale of the Democracity show from the 1939 World's Fair.*

THE American city of today is part Bel Geddes, part Levitt, part Le Corbusier. It is to a large extent the world promised in Futurama. The optimism is gone, and we have the fragments of many utopias. We have skyscrapers in number and height that would impress the cliff dwellers of the 1920s, and we have highways that outnumber the motorways proposed by Bel Geddes. And certainly no one would proclaim American cities as a wonder of the age.

In a speech he made in California in 1962, Lewis Mumford put the American city in perspective:

"Ever since I visited the ancient Italian town of Pompeii, buried under the ashes of Vesuvius in A.D. 79, I have found myself comparing the dead city that has been brought to life there with the seemingly live cities we are living in—or more often trying to get away from—in America. This comparison continues to haunt me.

"The landscape around Pompeii is not too different from that of many parts of California; the vineyards and the olive groves and wheat fields in Roman times were no more productive. Yet this little provincial town, of some 25,000 inhabitants, produced such an orderly and coherent and aesthetically animated life that even in its ruined state it gives a less ruinous impression than the central areas of most American cities of ten times that population. . . .

"When one compares the noble form of Pompeii with the jumbled junk-edged surroundings of San Francisco's own Civic Center, when one compares the amount of space and fine building given to Pompeii's temples, its markets, its law courts, its public baths, its stadium, its handsome theater . . . one realizes that American towns far more wealthy and populous than Pompeii do not, except in very rare cases, have anything like this kind of civic equipment, even in makeshift form."

Why does a ruined Roman town present a more orderly cityscape than a living American city? The moral Mumford draws is that we "have fallen in love with the machine," and we have come to be governed by mass production, standardization, automation, and quantitative excess—all terms that could describe many of the skyscraper utopias. (Some of the skyscrapers are lined up as if they were rolling off an assembly line. In fact, several architects took the assembly line as a model when laying out "linear" cities.) We believe that the latest invention will solve all our problems. In a republic that celebrates the inventing spirit, the city was just another invention a few patents down the road from perfectibility.

Our approach to cities was highlighted by a recent symposium concerning Minneapolis, Minnesota. Here is a city that most agree is a success. Minneapolis brings to mind a clean city, overarched with blue skies. It brings to mind Philip Johnson's combined office and hotel high rise, the IDS Center with its indoor town square, the city's much-noted skyway system, the fantastic parks, and, of course, the fact that people who live there love it. But at a closer look, Minneapolis is disappointing. The symposium was excerpted in *Design Quarterly 125* (1984). The photos in the issue show what a gap-toothed downtown Minneapolis really has. There are elegant glass towers and acres of parking lots, with many streets covered by a big project or two, but few streets with many little buildings and few streets with anyone walking. The city appeared in these photos as if painted by a photo-realist: the hard-edged glitter of parked autos and glass towers that serve to announce an emptiness.

The issue begins with the famous quote by Daniel Burnham to make no little plans, to make big plans. After examining in detail several new buildings in Minneapolis, it ends with a discussion in which Jaquelin Robertson, Dean of the School of Architecture at the University of Virginia, says: "We must really abandon the hope that architecture is going to make good cities, and that the better the design of buildings, the better the cities. It's just

13.   Apple trees under glass: an experimental farm of the future in the Futurama exhibit. "The apple tree of Tomorrow, abloom under its inviolate hood, makes you stop and wonder. How will the little boy climb it? Where will the little bird build its nest?" wrote E. B. White.

clearly not true. There are beautifully designed buildings all over the country. Architecture is everywhere and the architects are becoming celebrities. But cities are getting worse."

The American city is a carnival of variety, each building straining for novelty, Robertson says, but there is little thought given to how all this might form any kind of workable public space.

"Although there is architecture everywhere in Minneapolis, there is as yet no city. There is the residue of an old city, and the promise of a city to come. But the new city that one walks through is really a kind of *Sweet's Catalog* of spare parts. There's absolutely nothing about it that relates to any historical concept of any culture in the history of urbanism.

"Physically we don't have a clue yet about how the standard parts might go together. Until we have even the crudest blueprint of what cities are, we won't make them. We'll continue to build. We have lots of built-up places, but we're not building cities—not *this culture*, not yet."

W̲E persist in looking at the parts and not the whole, looking for the next invention that will save us or looking to outmoded inventions. We still love the skyscraper.

There has been much talk lately of the superskyscraper, the 200-story or taller building. Engineers have gathered to discuss the prospects at a symposium held by the *Engineering News Record* in 1983 (the same year conferees in Minneapolis were decrying the lack of a cohesive downtown) and in 1986 at a Chicago conference, "The Second Century of the Skyscraper."

The technology to build higher is available, and the engineers have readied detailed plans. Wind resistance is the major problem at heights of a half-mile to a mile. At cloud level, a tower would have to be braced against steady winds of 90 miles per hour. An improperly braced building would sway, water in toilets would slosh, and office workers could become seasick. The engineers have come up with a diverse group of solutions. One plan would use bundles of steel tubes. Technically, it could be built to 500 stories, a mile high. The triangular structure would require a building site sixteen blocks long. ("It could single handedly revive the U.S. steel business," says the designer.) Another engineer envisions a closely packed cluster of skyscrapers, tethered together at great heights to steady themselves against the wind. And one engineer sees the phasing out of tall towers in favor of "tall cities." A steel framework the size of a small city would be laid out. The towers would rise from this frame and be connected at many different levels. (It is a proposal reminiscent of the future city portrayed in *King's Views of New York.*)

What are the consequences of building so high? There would be an immense energy demand to pump water and to heat and cool offices one-half mile up in the sky. Fire codes would have

14.   One mile straight up. The 500-story skyscraper is technically feasible. "You never know," says one architect, "how high developers may ask you to go these days."

to be rewritten. The wait for an elevator could rival the wait for a bus. On the ground, what of the shadows and down-drafts from the building? Never mind. If the economics are not there, the "egonomics" are. Some corporate client will want to be the tallest, and the engineers are ready. (This is how the World Trade Center came to be—for a time—the world's tallest. The Port Authority of New York had spent years making voluminous studies and the tower design was well underway when a public relations employee had a rush-hour reverie: The towers were already big—so why not the biggest? Where economics gave out, "egonomics" took over.)

Some of the engineers do see the foolishness of this sky's-the-limit pursuit. As things stand now, perhaps 90 percent to 95 percent of all buildings constructed do not operate as designed, says Israel A. Naman, an engineer-consultant. Poorly installed heating and air conditioning are the usual problems making the workplace uncomfortable. (As always, automation, computers, and new devices are held out as the solution.)

The consequences of going to 200 stories far outweigh routine matters of heating and cooling. "The idea that a single individual should be allowed to make all these decisions privately is absurd," says a leading skyscraper engineer, William Le Messurier. "We wouldn't let anybody do a dam that might flood a city by himself, or design a nuclear plant by himself—why a 200 story building?"

BEYOND questions of technology and advertisement, the idea of building higher has a great fascination. Even though the skyscraper has entered its "second century," it still represents the future. And like the five million who saw the Futurama show and the millions who saw the Great Big Beautiful Tomorrow show, we possess a faith in the future.

There is one story told by Henry Luce, maker and master of the *Time* magazine empire, that underscores all the schemes for tomorrow.

He told of a meeting in his office with the great photographer Margaret Bourke-White. The year is 1954. If Bourke-White wanted to see him, it was because she had "some big and probably wild and expensive project to propose." Bourke-White had traveled the globe for *Life,* from the North Pole to Africa. "When she came into my office she proceeded in a matter-of-fact manner to register her request. She wanted a promise that it would be she and no other who would have the assignment to go to the moon. Taking her quite seriously, I said yes." This is, mind you, three years before Sputnik. Luce reports this conversation in a 1955 book, *The Fabulous Future: America in 1980.* (No irony was intended. The book is itself a monument to the "future faith.")

Bourke-White may have been early, but this is the direction

15.   Cleaning the slate. The tangled streets of old London are wiped away in this cartoon from a book published shortly after the end of World War II. The City of Tomorrow would free itself from the "outmoded street." (The MIT Press)

we are accustomed to looking toward. Back during the first moon landing, a New York area radio station held a contest: first prize was a trip to Hawaii or a reserved seat on the first Pan Am Clipper to the moon. How to choose? Defer pleasure now for the ride of a lifetime? Many people forsook Hawaii, yesterday's paradise, and booked themselves to the moon. (To this day, 90,002 Americans still hold reservations for the Pan Am Clipper to the moon.)

It seems as if we have been deceiving ourselves. While we have been waiting for a Great Big Beautiful Tomorrow and planning mile-high towers, another future has crept in unnoticed.

THE city of the future is a shantytown. Throughout the world, it is known by many names, *ranchos* in Venezuela, *barriadas* in Peru, *ravelas* in Brazil, *bidonvilles* in the French-speaking world, *ishish* in the Mideast. In Mexico, the name for these cities translates to "Lost Cities," and to governments everywhere they are unplanned cities. Whatever their name, by some estimates they will soon house the majority of the world's population. Here is the future we never counted on, where life is nasty, brutish, and long.

The world's population is doubling every thirty years. The world's urban population is doubling every fifteen years. And the size of these shadow settlements engulfing the official city is doubling every seven and one-half years. Mexico City has grown from 4.5 million in 1960 to 19 million today. It's headed toward 30 million by the year 2000. In Mexico City's Lost Cities, the poorest of the poor live in caves carved out of mountains of trash. For such people, utopia can be found in a bucket of clean water, and the wonder world of a future city would include a roof and a clean place to sleep.

The shantytown future is a distressing place to end up. It is

25

like emerging from a darkened movie theater and having to squint your eyes against the light of day. We have been watching a show promising us a serene future that was, above all else, planned. We would be like the marionettes dancing on the stage; our cities would get newer and newer as we gracefully aged. The wonders of our own devising would unfold before us as we became wiser.

A brief, simplified show of the City of Tomorrow placed on that rotating stage could take place with the same marionettes (here architects, planners, engineers, politicians) singing, "It's—a—great—big—beautiful—tomorrow." And the stage would turn.

There would be a quick introductory scene while the curtain was still down. Pictures would be flashed of London's Victorian slums and New York's Lower East Side in the century's first decade, accompanied by words from Dickens, Henry Mayhew, and Jacob Riis.

The curtain would shortly rise to applause—a stage bathed in green light. Birds singing. Our marionettes out for a stroll. Ebenezer Howard's Garden City. The stage would turn; we would find our marionettes basking in the sunshine of Le Corbusier's Radiant City. There would be brilliant white towers and a feeling that the marionettes had great power at their disposal. So it would go as the marionettes flew about Frank Lloyd Wright's Broadacre City in their aircars, in one scene, and in another looked down from the heights of their skyscraper home in the clouds. In still another, they would race through the "World of 1960" at 100 miles an hour in teardrop-shaped cars. There could be yet more scenes—there are a great number of future cities on tap. We would applaud at the end, happily, "filled with a strong sweet poison in the blood," as E. B. White said of his Futurama visit, snug in the knowledge that the future was getting better by every minute and that we were being looked after.

Leaving the theater, we might cast a glance back at the stage and see the pictures of squalor again as they set up for a new show. In fact, we would have risen from our seats too soon. That first scene is the end of the show. That is the future we missed—the future city as the past city. Ahead of us we have the past, behind us, the future.

All these planned cities were responses to the excesses of the nineteenth-century city. In 1900, only 14 percent of the world's population lived in cities. By the century's end, more than half of all humanity will live in cities. We face the problems of the twenty-first century, and all we have in hand are a few proposals from the century before.

In the poor nations, there is one scene common to all their cities: new skyscrapers—banks, luxury hotels—towers of glass, and creamy concrete and, at their base, stretching away in the distance, the slums of the Lost City.

16. *An international capital city. Inspired by the worldwide peace movement, Hendrik Christian Andersen advocated a World Centre. The sculptor began his project in 1904 and later formed a World Conscience Society in 1913. French architect Ernest Hebrard drew the plans in the grand manner of the École des Beaux-Arts. The planned city covered about 10 square miles. Its centerpiece was a central Avenue des Nations, which ran from the sea to the Tower of Progress. There were large centers for sports, art, music, science, and justice set along radiating avenues and surrounded by parks.*

THIS is where we end. Down from the God's-eye view of the city plans, down from the mountains of skyscrapers. Away from all the rhetoric exhorting us forward. In all this, we have lost what the city has meant throughout history. City air makes free, was the medieval saying.

What the city can be—what should guide us as we face the Lost City—was expressed best by the poet and Nobel Laureate Czeslaw Milosz. It is right that a poet should have the last word. We have heard from the architects, planners, and statisticians.

In his autobiography, Milosz recalled his arrival in Paris, one summer morning in 1931:

"Four or five O'Clock. Grey-pink, iridescent air like the enamel inside a shell. We inhaled Paris with open nostrils, cutting across it on foot, diagonally from north toward the Seine. The moist flowers, the vegetables, the coffee, the damp pavement, the mingling odors of night and day. Where the wide sidewalks changed into a market place, we took pleasure in submerging ourselves in the human stream, its color, movement, gestures, and glances. We lost count of the streets, we forgot about our own existence . . . the promise was infinite, it was the promise of life."

Yesterday

Living and Working in the Smoke

To-day

Living in the Suburbs – Working in the Smoke

To-morrow

Living & Working in the Sun at WELWYN GARDEN CITY

17. *"Living and working in the sun." Advertisement for Welwyn Garden City, the second garden city built by Ebenezer Howard and his followers in 1920. A movement that had hoped to plant one hundred garden cities in England had to settle for two.*

Part II

THE REFORMING SPIRIT

WITH the coming of the Industrial Revolution, at the start of the nineteenth century, the world began to pour into the cities. Slums spread, and reformers began to catalogue the evils of life there. Rivers had become dumps for "wagonloads of poisons from dye houses and bleachyards." Worker houses, as in Homestead, Pennsylvania, were built right up against the factory, often on a landfill of ashes, in the tumult of the noise and smell from the factory. In the bigger cities, living conditions were worse. In

18. *"Living and working in the smoke." Homestead, Pennsylvania.*

Manchester, England, a study found but one toilet for 212 inhabitants. In Liverpool, another study found that more than one-quarter of the population was living underground. In close quarters, disease spread and infant mortality soared amid the rats, lice, and bedbugs, the typhus and smallpox. Things were so bad that one reformer, Herbert Spencer, pleaded with parents to allow their children to eat fruit.

Against this backdrop, people began to think and dream of ways to create better cities. There were plans to bring a magisterial order to the city in the City Beautiful Movement; plans to diffuse the city in Ebenezer Howard's Garden City and Frank Lloyd Wright's Broadacre City; and plans to rework the city, making it more hygienic, in Le Corbusier's Radiant City and Tony Garnier's Cité Industrielle.

These plans sought to reform the entire system; they were about more than just aligning streets and buildings. As Le Corbusier remarked in *The City of Tomorrow and Its Planning*, "Town planning has now become a sort of dumping ground for every difficult and unresolved problem, such as the birth rate, the social equilibrium, alcoholism, crime, the moral of the great city, civic affairs and so forth."

THE CIVIC IMPULSE

THE City Beautiful movement was part of "the world-wide civic battle between Ugliness and Beauty," wrote C. M. Robinson in 1901. Robinson, who coined the phrase, "the City Beautiful," was a tireless promoter: "Something very like religious fervor can be put into the zeal for city beauty, sustaining it through long patience and slow work."

The City Beautiful reached its fullest expression in Daniel Burnham's *Plan of Chicago,* which was published in 1909. Backed by private initiative, it was the first comprehensive plan for a large American city. The plan laid out sweeping changes for Chicago: widened avenues, lakefront parks, museums, consolidated rail lines.

19. A noble city hall for Chicago. The central administration building as shown in the Plan of Chicago *would house a less-than-holy city government in a domed building of holy proportions. "Rising from the plain upon which Chicago rests, its effect may be compared to that of St. Peter's at Rome," wrote Daniel Burnham and Edward Bennett in the* Plan of Chicago *(1909). Detail. (The Art Institute of Chicago)*

The plan's backers brought their business sense to city planning. They energetically sold the idea to the public. A 93-page pamphlet outlining the plan was mailed to 165,000 property owners (addressed to the "Owners of Chicago"), slide lectures were given to full auditoriums, and, in the infancy of the motion picture, a two-reel movie was made. Pamphlets were sent to ministers with "seed thoughts for sermons," and a version of the plan was required reading for all eighth-grade students in Chicago. In the following twenty years, the City of Chicago spent $300 million on improvements suggested by the plan.

Daniel Burnham, the architect of the plan and of other civic improvements for Washington, D.C., San Francisco, and elsewhere, portrayed the spirit of the civic movement in his famous pronouncement of 1907:

"Make no little plans; they have no magic to stir men's blood and probably themselves will not be realized. Make big plans; aim high in hope and work, remembering that a noble, logical diagram once recorded will never die, but long after we are gone will be a living thing, asserting itself with ever-growing insistency. Remember that our sons and grandsons are going to do things that would stagger us. Let your watchword be order and your beacon beauty."

20. *City hall rising in the civic center plaza, flanked by county and federal government buildings. The civic center would "typify the permanence of the city," wrote Burnham and Bennett. "Such a group of buildings as Chicago should and may possess would be for all time to come a distinction to the city. It would be what the Acropolis was to Athens, or the Forum to Rome, and what St. Mark's Square is to Venice—the very embodiment of civic life." (The Art Institute of Chicago)*

*21.   A view looking down on
the civic center plaza. (The Art
Institute of Chicago)*

22.   *A view showing the plaza in relationship to Lake Michigan. (The Art Institute of Chicago)*

23.   *(facing page) The civic center shrinks in size as the rest of Chicago comes into view. The broad, radiating avenues laid over the gridwork of Chicago are part of the Beaux-Arts plan. (The Art Institute of Chicago)*

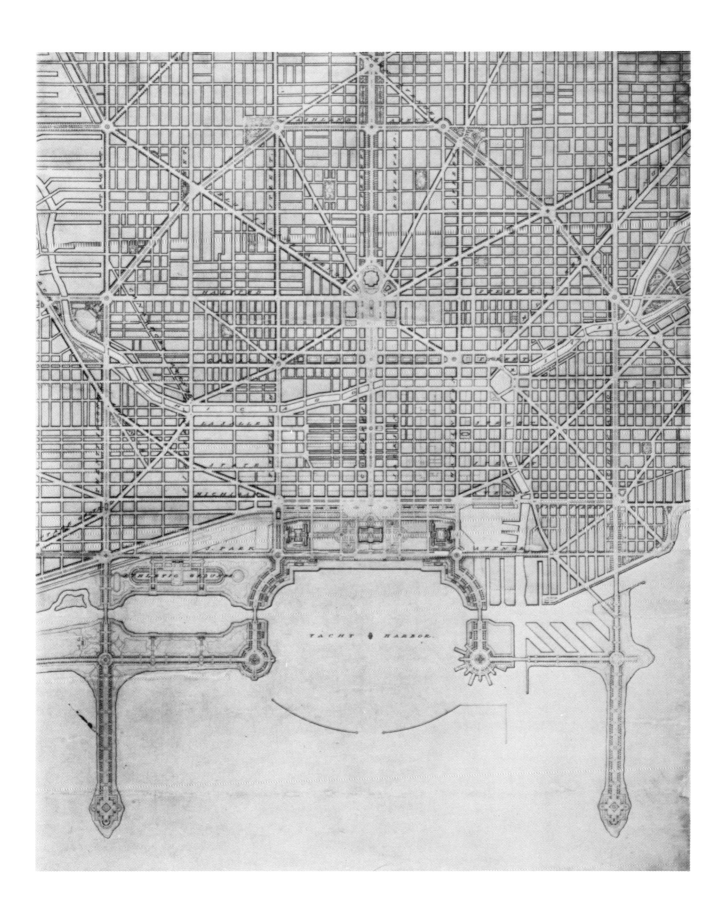

THE GARDEN CITY

A London stenographer, Ebenezer Howard, was always trying his hand at inventions. His formal education ended at age 14, and by all accounts, he was "the mildest and most unassuming of men," a man who could easily disappear in a crowd. In 1898, he published *To-morrow: A Peaceful Path to Real Reform.* This slim book, known under its 1902 title, *Garden Cities of To-morrow,* has, said Lewis Mumford, "done more than any other single book to guide the modern town planning movement and to alter its objectives."

Howard proposed a marriage of town and country—not garden suburbs, not a town in the country but the advantages of both. Towns would be of limited size, and all land would be held in common. The towns would provide industrial employment carefully laid out at the outer ring, green parks at center, and extensive surrounding agricultural lands. When the town reached its population limit, a new town at some distance would be established. Eventually, there would be a ring of satellite towns around the central city.

"Each inhabitant . . . though in one sense living in a town of small size, would be in reality living in, and enjoy all the advantages of, a great and most beautiful city; and yet, all the fresh delights of the country—field, hedgerow and woodland—not prim parks and gardens merely—would be within a very few minutes' walk or ride," wrote Howard. "And *because the people in their collective capacity own the land* . . . on which this beautiful group of cities is built, the public buildings, the churches, the schools and universities, the libraries, picture galleries, theatres, would be on a scale of magnificence which no city in the world whose land is in pawn to private individuals can afford."

24.   A "group of slumless, smokeless cities" as drawn by Ebenezer Howard in 1898, showing six garden cities and a central city connected by canals and railways. Howard intended his drawings to be used as a diagram, not a specific site plan.

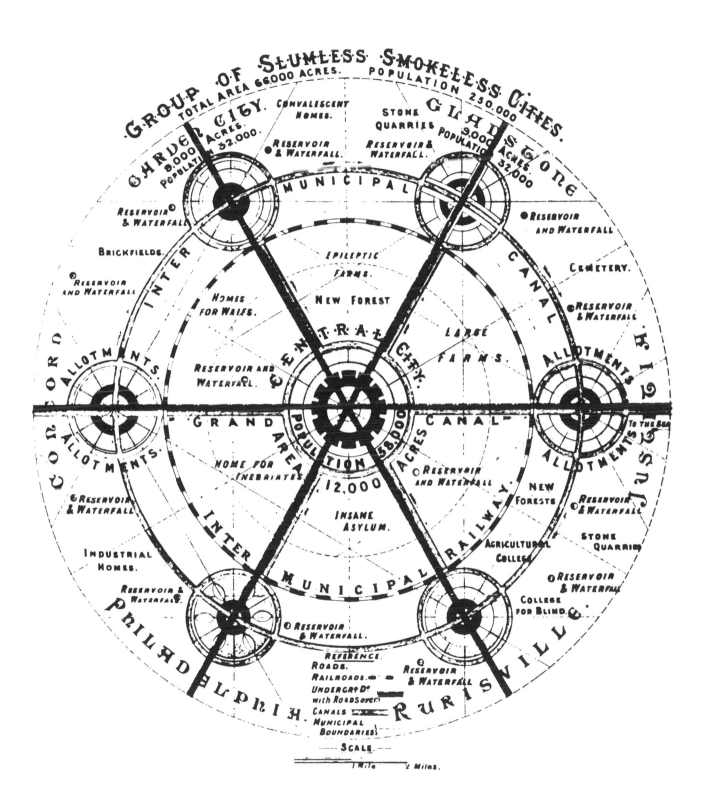

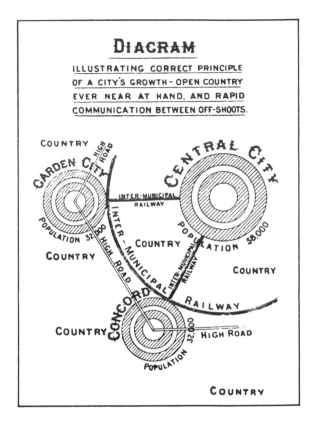

DIAGRAM

ILLUSTRATING CORRECT PRINCIPLE
OF A CITY'S GROWTH - OPEN COUNTRY
EVER NEAR AT HAND, AND RAPID
COMMUNICATION BETWEEN OFF-SHOOTS.

25. and 26. Left, "The correct principle of a city's growth." Once a garden city reached a population of 32,000, another city at a proper distance would be established. Below, the garden city surrounded by farmland. Each city would occupy 1,000 acres, surrounded by 5,000 acres of agricultural land.

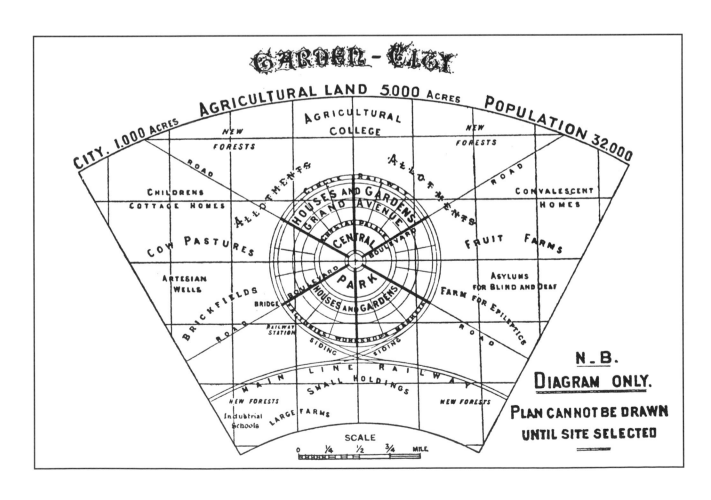

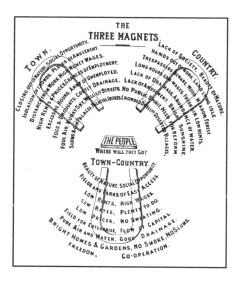

27. and 28.   *Below, the garden city close up. At the city center, a three-acre garden surrounded by civic buildings, further surrounded by a central park. A shopping district encircled this. Housed in a "Crystal Palace," a glass arcade, this may be the earliest proposal for a shopping mall. A "Grand Avenue," 420 feet wide, separated the residential area from the factories. At left, the three magnets. Howard laid out the advantages and disadvantages of town and country life. His garden cities would combine the advantages of both, producing a town–country magnet. "Town and country **must be married** and out of this joyous union will spring a new hope, a new life, a new civilization."*

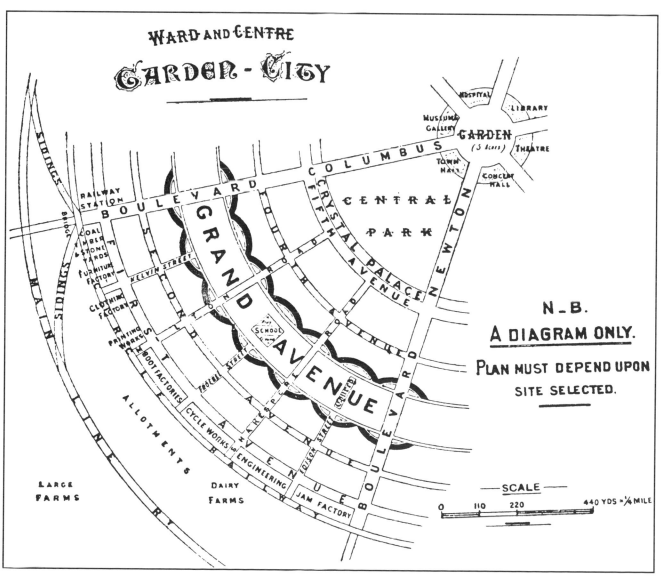

ROAD · & · RAIL · COMMUNICATIONS ·

DIAGRAM · OF · TOWN · PLAN · SHEWING · ZONES

SHOPS · PUBLIC · BUILDINGS · OPEN · SPACES · ETC.

WELWYN GARDEN · CITY ·

LOUIS · DE · SOISSONS · ARIBA
SADG · ARCHITECT

Scale of Chains.

Scale of feet

Residential Areas   Factory Areas.   Open Spaces   Shopping Areas.

40

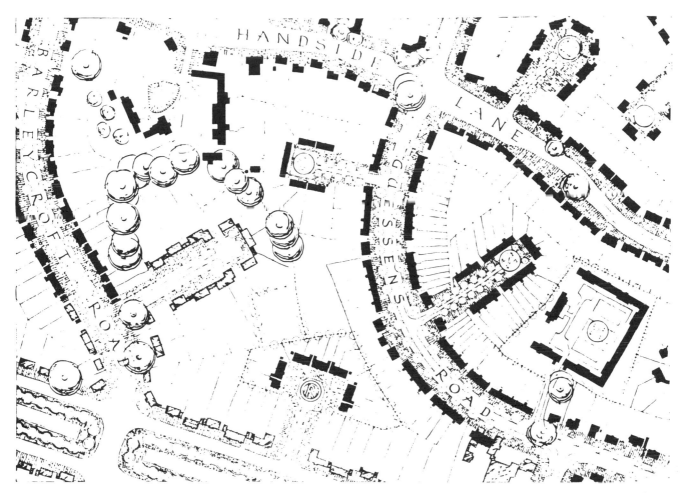

29. and 30.   Left, the garden
city realized. In Welwyn, the
second garden city, the agricultural belt had shrunk from
Howard's projected 5,000 acres to
608 acres, and a population of
40,000 to 50,000 was planned.
While the civic center was never
built, the factories did flourish.
Above, Louis de Soisson drew the
master plan in 1920, introducing
the cul-de-sac.

WELWYN GARDEN CITY

400 ft

In the Hertfordshire Highlands

Twenty-one miles from King's Cross

The New Town for Residence & Industry.

IT is not good to waste two hours daily in trains buses and trams to and from the workshop, leaving no time nor energy for leisure or recreation

AT Welwyn Garden City a mans house will be near his work in a pure and healthy atmosphere

He will have time & energy after his work is done for leisure & recreation

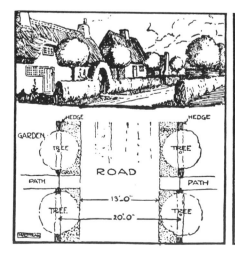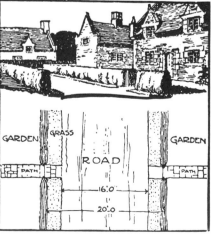

*31. and 32.	George Bernard Shaw said that the English nation owed Ebenezer Howard an Earldom for Letchworth and a Dukedom for Welwyn. Howard was knighted in 1927. Below, architects Raymond Unwin and Barry Parker evoked the idealized English village in their designs for Letchworth (1903).*

*33. and 34.	(facing page) A successful failure. The Russell Sage Foundation set out in 1912 to build Forest Hill Gardens as a model village of lower-income housing. Despite efforts to keep costs down, its proximity to Manhattan drove land values up, and it quickly became the upper-middle-class neighborhood it is today. While a pleasing place to live, as an experiment in lower-class housing it was a failure.*

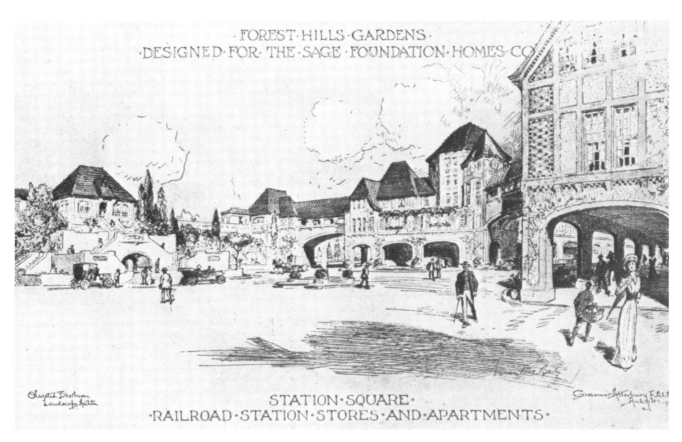

FOREST·HILLS·GARDENS·
DESIGNED·FOR·THE·SAGE·FOUNDATION·HOMES·CO·

STATION·SQUARE·
RAILROAD·STATION·STORES·AND·APARTMENTS·

BIRDS EYE VIEW

35.　A whimsical view of *Forest Hill Gardens. The curved streets that break the city's grid are in the English garden suburb tradition. Grosvenor Atterbury's design made it particularly attractive to the upper middle class.*

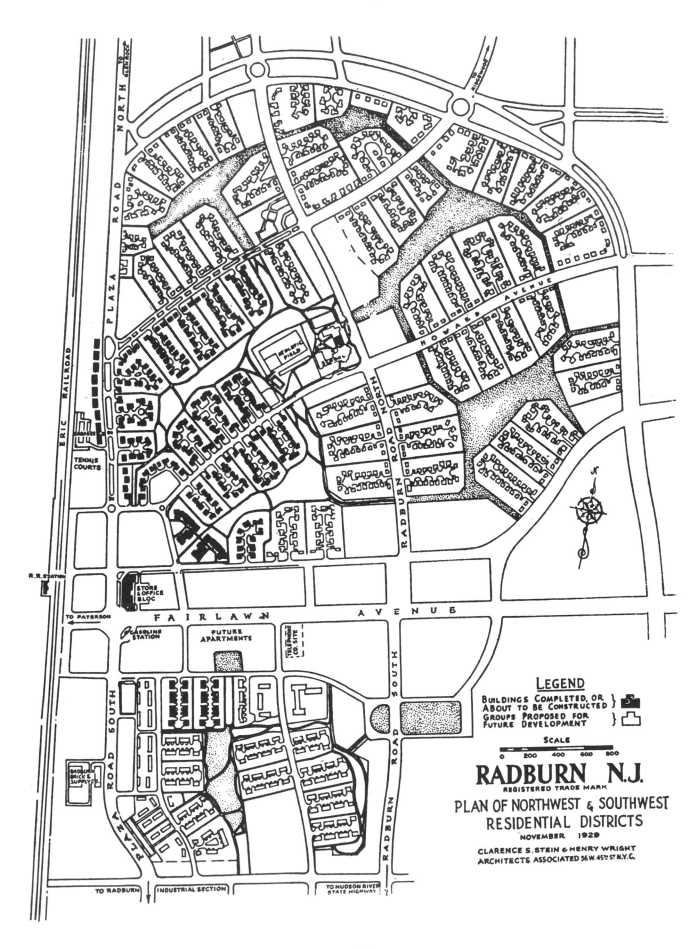

LEGEND

BUILDINGS COMPLETED, OR ABOUT TO BE CONSTRUCTED

GROUPS PROPOSED FOR FUTURE DEVELOPMENT

SCALE
0 200 400 600 800

RADBURN N.J.
REGISTERED TRADE MARK

PLAN OF NORTHWEST & SOUTHWEST RESIDENTIAL DISTRICTS
NOVEMBER 1929

CLARENCE S. STEIN & HENRY WRIGHT
ARCHITECTS ASSOCIATED 56 W. 45TH ST N.Y.C.

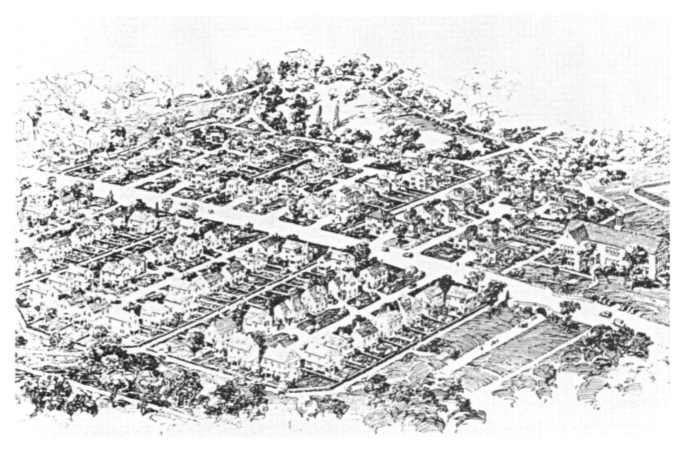

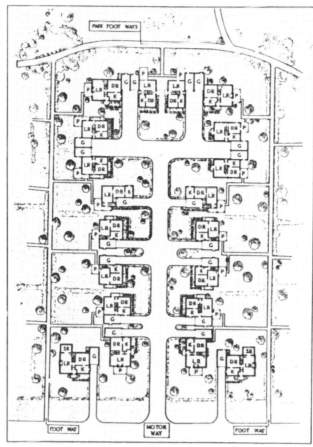

36. (facing page) A modest future that might have been. Clarence Stein's and Henry Wright's 1928 plan for Radburn, New Jersey, could have become the model for suburban development in America. The Depression hindered the full development of the plan, and architecture critics derided the conservative Georgian architecture of the houses. When the suburban boom blossomed after World War II, Radburn as a model was ignored by builders, who were reluctant to give over so much space to common land, but admired by planning professionals.

37. and 38. The layout of Radburn. The houses front on a cul-de-sac and back onto a greensward with extensive footways. Radburn residents could travel unhindered by the motorcar.

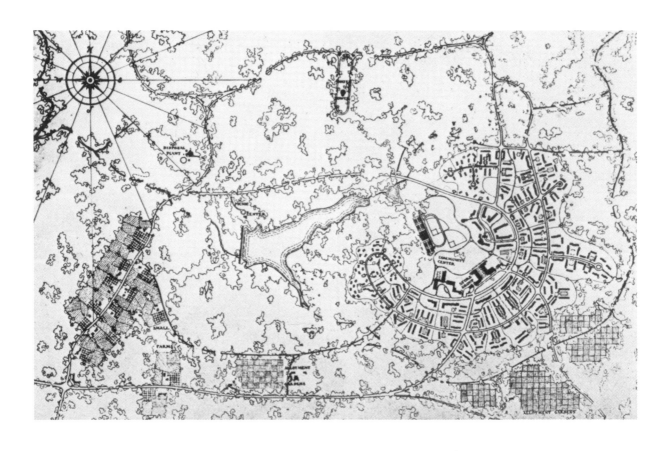

PLAN OF COMMERCIAL CENTER · GREENBELT, MARYLAND.

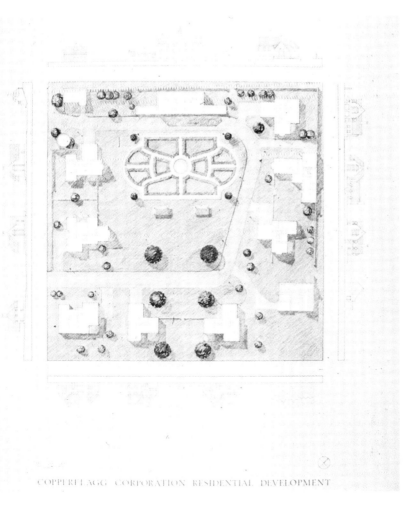

COPPERFLAGG CORPORATION RESIDENTIAL DEVELOPMENT

39. and 40. (facing page) *The "Ultimate Town," the "new city ready to serve a better age," Greenbelt, Maryland, was a bold exercise in government planning in 1937. There was low-income housing for 17,000 people set among pedestrian paths, underpasses, and cul-de-sacs. Attacked by some as "communistic boondoggles," the New Deal town building program was quickly curtailed. Of one hundred envisioned cities, only three were built.*

41. *The romantic present. Copperflagg, a residential development on an old Staten Island estate, is typical of many plans that aspire to the Tuxedo Park romance of the pre-World War suburbs, when the suburbs belonged to the rich.*

49

BROADACRE CITY

To look at the plan of any great city is to look at the cross-section of some fibrous tumor," wrote Frank Lloyd Wright in one of his numerous antiurban pronouncements. He believed that the city reduced the citizen to "a vendor of gadgetry, a salesman dealing for profit in human frailities."

"Even the small town is too large," he wrote in *The Future of Architecture.* "It will gradually merge into the general non-urban development. Ruralism as distinguished from urbanism, is American and truly democratic."

The automobile, Wright said, would restore America to the landscape envisioned by Thomas Jefferson. Wright's Broadacre City would be inhabited by self-sufficient farmers and independent businessmen.

Laid out on a grid, each family would have its acre of land and be free from the enslaving rent of city landlords. These independent homesteads would be supplemented by small factories. All these small farmers and manufacturers would trade their goods at the Roadside Market, where each would have a booth. There was a community center as well, but, unlike other garden city plans, there was no central downtown area. Travel by automobile united the inhabitants. The one sign of status Wright allowed in his Usonian houses was the number of garages a person could have, with five being the top.

"Broadacre city is everywhere or nowhere. It is the country itself come alive as a truly great city."

42.   *The city diffused. "When every man, woman, and child may be born to put his feet on his own acres, then democracy will have been realized," wrote Frank Lloyd Wright. Broadacre City was Wright's answer to the evils of centralized wealth in the big city. The automobile, Wright believed, provided a means to create a landscape inhabited by independent farmers and business people.*

43.   *A street scene in Broad-acre City. The cars and helicopters are Wright's own designs.*

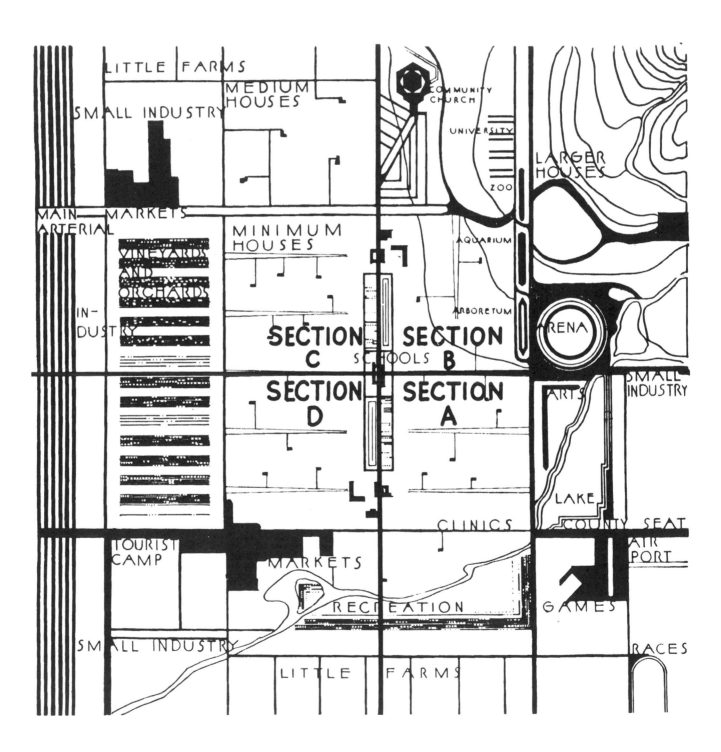

LITTLE FARMS

MEDIUM HOUSES

SMALL INDUSTRY

COMMUNITY CHURCH

UNIVERSITY

LARGER HOUSES

ZOO

MAIN ARTERIAL

MARKETS

MINIMUM HOUSES

VINEYARDS AND ORCHARDS

AQUARIUM

IN-DUSTRY

ARBORETUM

ARENA

SECTION C

SECTION B

SCHOOLS

SMALL INDUSTRY

SECTION D

SECTION A

ARTS

LAKE

CLINICS

COUNTY SEAT

TOURIST CAMP

MARKETS

AIR PORT

GAMES

RECREATION

SMALL INDUSTRY

LITTLE FARMS

RACES

45. *A scene for celebrations. The circus for county fairs and pageants as seen in the Broadacre City model. Behind the stadium stands a "monumental pole" for announcing festivals. The model was exhibited in 1935 at Rockefeller Center and elsewhere around the country.*

THE RADIANT CITY

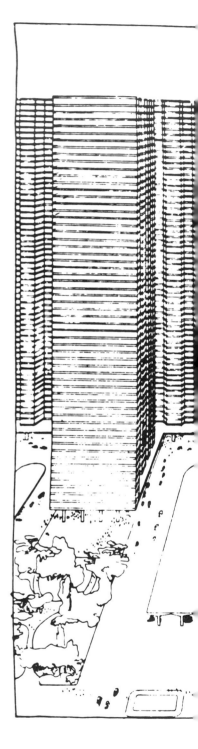

LE Corbusier told this story of how he came to design his first ideal city.

In 1922, he was asked by a small museum to prepare an exhibit on urbanism. "What do you mean by urbanism?" Le Corbusier asked.

"Well, it's a sort of street art," he was told, "for stores, signs, and the like; it includes such things as the ornamental glass knobs on railings."

"Fine," said Le Corbusier. "I shall design a great fountain, and behind it, place a city for three million people."

"A Contemporary City for Three Million People" was the first of several city plans by Le Corbusier. He believed in freeing the city from its crowded, unhygienic streets. He stated his ideas:

1. We must decongest the center of our cities.
2. We must augment their density.
3. We must increase the means for getting about.
4. We must increase parks and open spaces.

Le Corbusier refined his ideas in the Plan Voisin for Paris and the Radiant City. He wrote a "hymn to shake the sky" to his new city:

A new world: a high speed world.
A new life: the machine age.
A new ideal: use of the machine to liberate the individual.
A new daily round: productive, recuperative, joyful, healthy; the daily round of the machine age man in the Radiant City.
New cities for old.

56

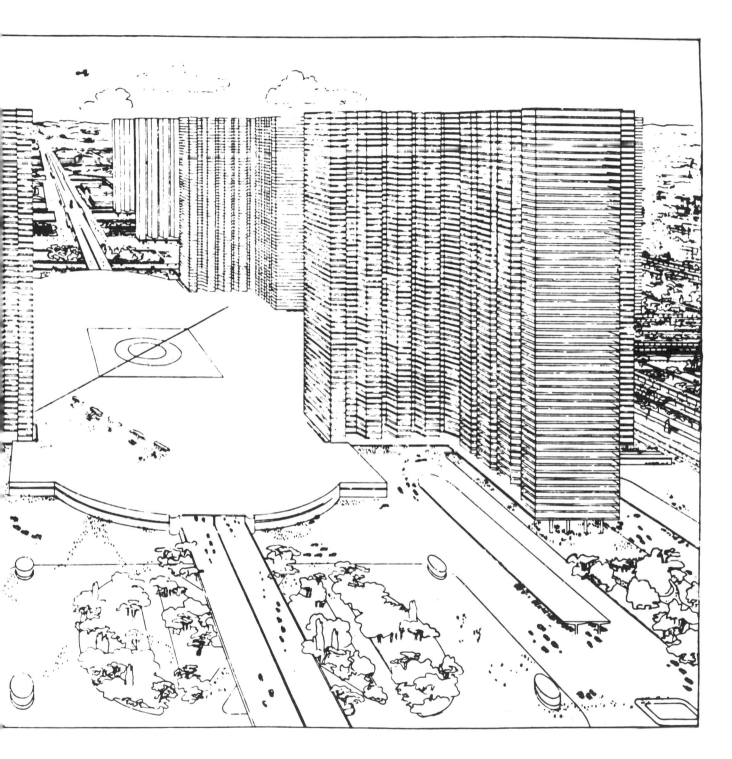

46. *The Radiant hour. Le Corbusier's first plan for an ideal city, the "Contemporary City for Three Million People" (1922). The building of this new city, Le Corbusier believed, would signal the arrival of the "radiant hour of harmony, construction and enthusiasm." He conceived of the city as an "ideal type" and saw himself as a "scientist in his laboratory . . . constructing a rigorous, theoretical structure." At the center of the Contemporary City are two dozen glass-and-steel, 60-story skyscrapers to accommodate 500,000 to 800,000 office workers. Even with such density, these towers cover less than 15 percent of the land.*

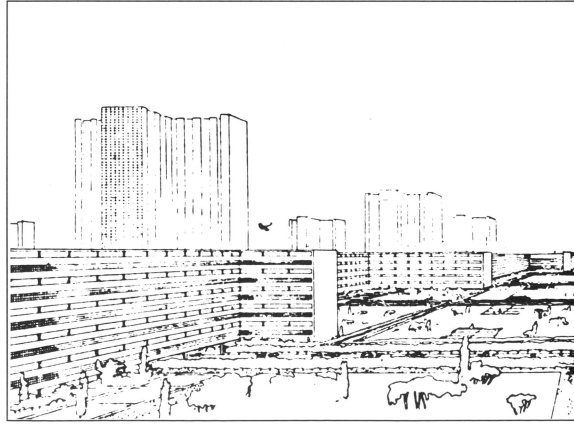

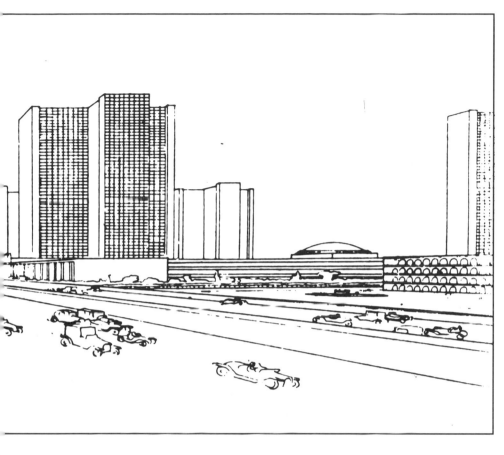

47.   *"The city that achieves speed, achieves success,"* wrote Le Corbusier. A superhighway forms the entryway leading directly to the center of the Contemporary City.

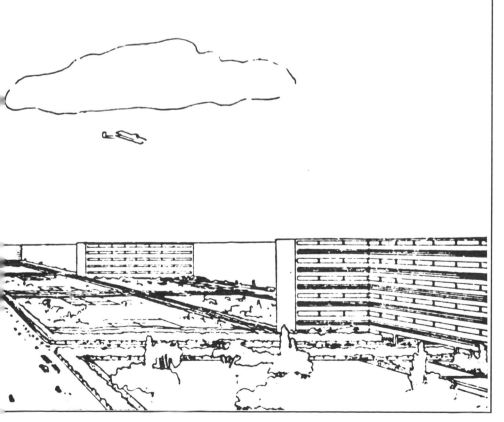

48.   *"Free, man tends to geometry,"* wrote Le Corbusier. *"The work of man is to put things in order."* The apartment blocks where the elite of the Contemporary City live show a well-ordered, geometric plan. The proletarians lived in satellite cities.

49.   "The death of the street."
A scale model of the Plan Voisin
(1925). Le Corbusier proposed his
towers for the heart of Paris. He
believed the old streets were dead
and unhygienic. At lower right are
the Seine and Île-de-la-Cité. Wrote
Le Corbusier: "In the name of the
beauty of Paris, you say, 'No!' In
the name of the beauty and destiny
of Paris, I say, 'Yes!' "

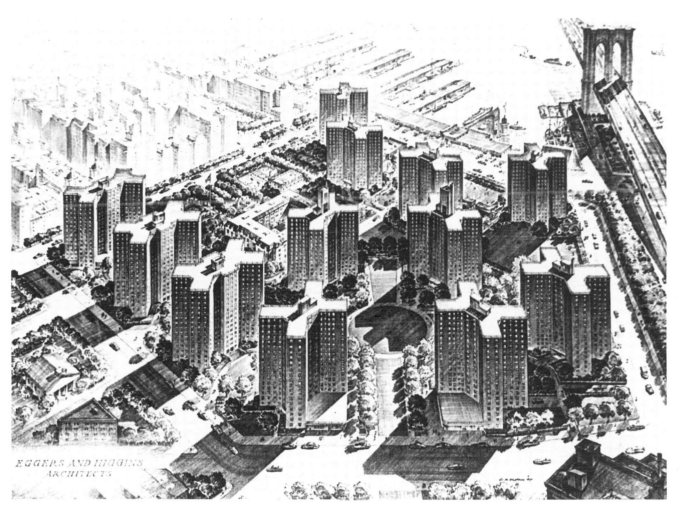

EGGERS AND HIGGINS
ARCHITECTS

50.   Le Corbusier's Plan
Voisin may be one of the most
influential ideas of the century.
Almost every city in the world
incorporates some fragment of his
idea of towers on the green.
Here, the Alfred E. Smith Houses
(1948), a low-income housing
project on the Lower East Side of
Manhattan. The Brooklyn Bridge
is to the right.

51.   (Overleaf) The Plan Voisin
seen in an overview drawn by Le
Corbusier. Five percent of the
area is built upon; 95 percent is
open. At center is a multilevel
traffic intersection. Le Corbusier
believed the auto had destroyed
the city and now would save it.

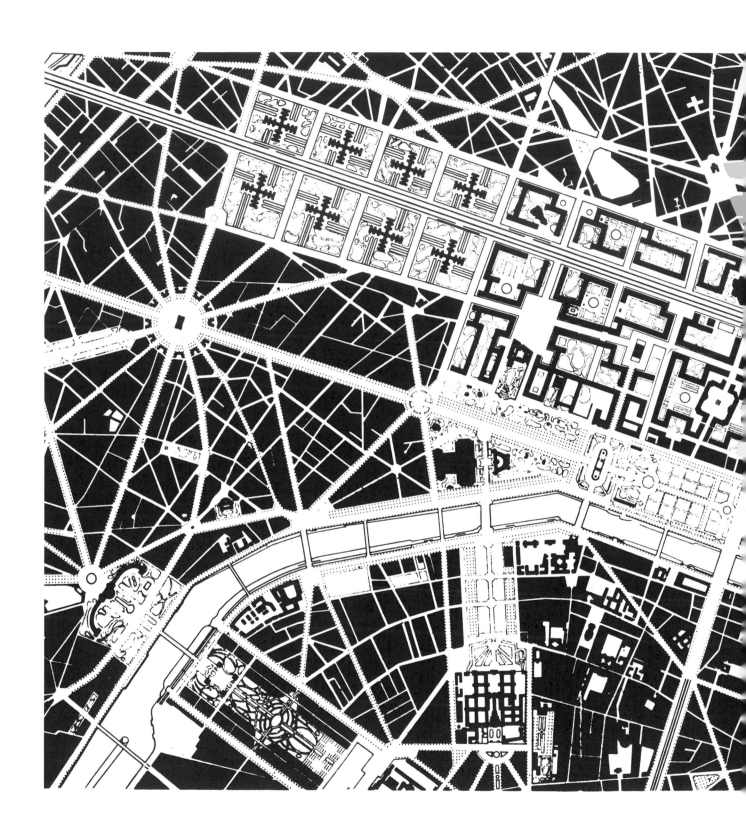

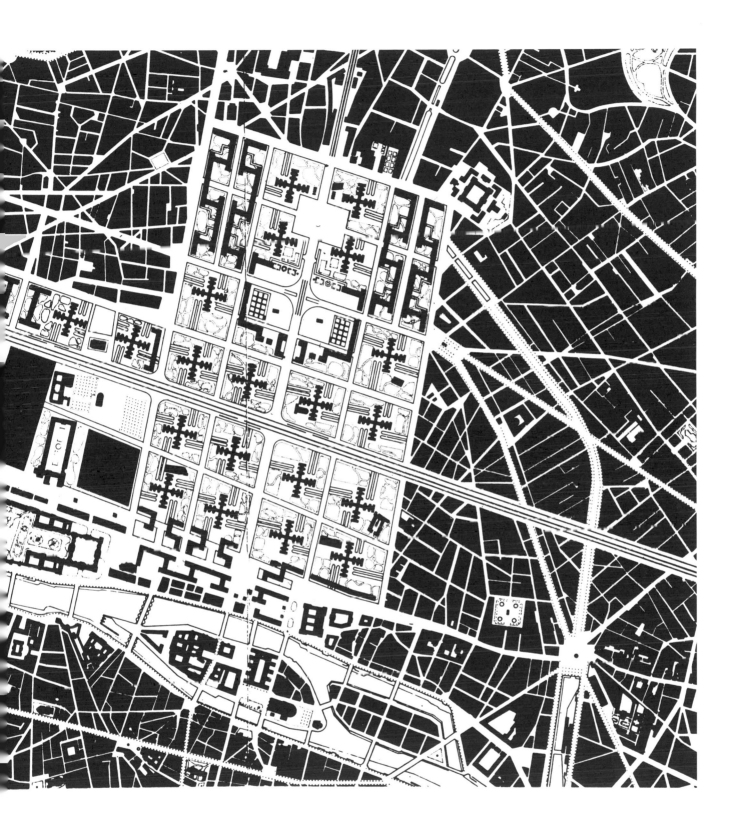

52.   The streets of old Paris
meet Le Corbusier's district of
towers. Toward the bottom of the
drawing are the Seine and Île-de-
la-Cité.

65

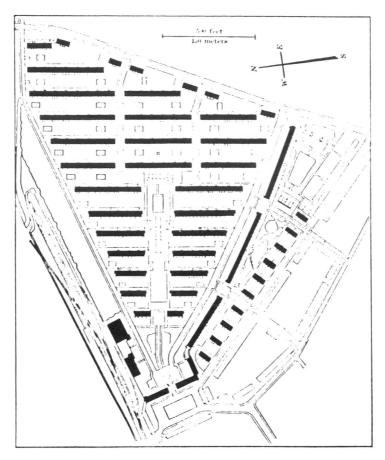

53.   The city rational. From the same era as Le Corbusier, this 1930 plan for the Bad Durrenberg district of Berlin was common of many plans in its rejection of the traditional street. The apartment blocks run approximately north–south and are spaced to allow maximum exposure to the sun.

54.   The city schematic. A surprising number of city plans began to resemble electronic schematics. Here is Cedric Price's Potteries Thinkbelt (1966). From bottom to top is a series of zones: railroad transfer, test-bed zone, flexible faculty zone, general trading zone, social exchange zone, and accommodation towers.

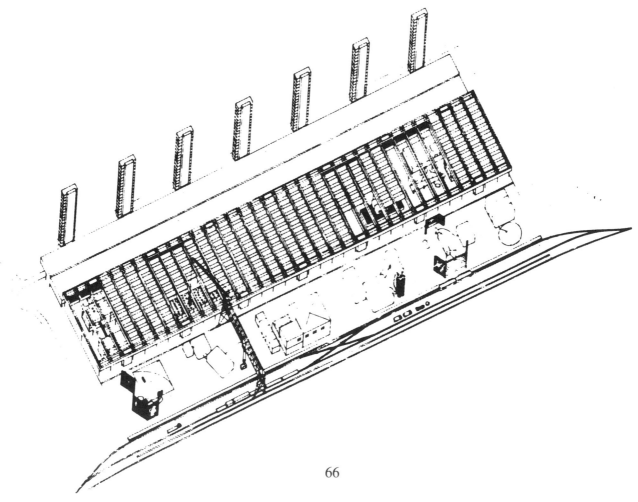

55.   *Rush City Reformed.*
*Inspired by the highway culture of
Los Angeles, Austrian émigré
architect Richard Neutra formu-
lated his city of the future (1923–
28). Here again, buildings are
arranged for maximum solar exposure and are limited to eleven
stories. The full area under each
building was devoted to parking
and traffic, but motor traffic was
excluded from the center district
and pedestrian ways were on the
second and third stories.*

56.   The "Ideal City." Ludwig Hilberseimer's 1920 drawing of a typical
modernist utopia: parallel rows of high-rise buildings with traffic and pedestrians separated. In the city, he said, "an enormously intensified rhythm of
life very rapidly represses every local and individual element." Hilberseimer
taught town planning at the Bauhaus and later at the Illinois Institute of Technology. (Museum of Modern Art)

LA CITÉ
INDUSTRIELLE

TONY Garnier mixed his training at the École des Beaux-Arts with socialist politics. Garnier was active in the radical socialist cause in Paris. When he won the coveted Prix de Rome in 1899, he spent his time designing an imaginary city, although such an unorthodox project was discouraged. After Garnier was appointed the city architect of Lyons, he continued to refine his plans. *Une Cité Industrielle* was published in 1917. Le Corbusier and others hailed Garnier's many innovative ideas.

Garnier had set himself the problem of designing an industrial city of 35,000 that would also be a humane place to live. The hypothetical city was worked out in great detail. It was a socialist city; all land was owned in common, and the city ran the businesses. It was a utopian city; although there were many public buildings, there was no court, police station, jail, or church. The low-rise city was oriented toward the sun and was energy self-sufficient, relying on a hydroelectric dam. The city was carefully zoned into public and residential quarters. Industry was located in its own quarter, close to the railroad and the harbor. The heights outside the city were reserved for hospitals, reflecting the emphasis on hygiene.

The plan was notable for its comprehensiveness and for the influence it was to have on a generation of modern architects.

57.   *The view of the factories of La Cité Industrielle. Boat sheds are built of reinforced concrete.*

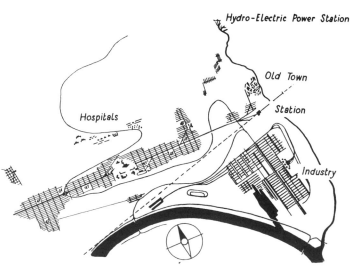

Hydro-Electric Power Station

Old Town

Hospitals

Station

Industry

58.   The plan for La Cité Industrielle (1904–17). The city was carefully zoned and laid out in relation to the sun, wind, and the railroad. It was planned for a site much like Garnier's native Lyons.

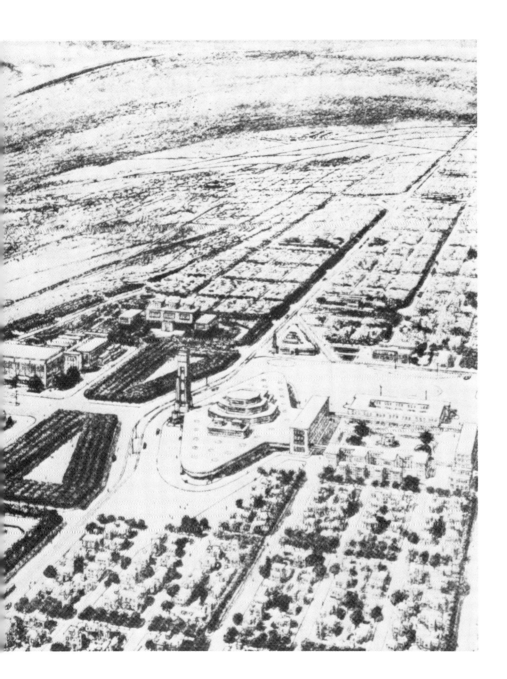

59.   The city center, dominated by a large assembly hall. The 3,000-seat assembly hall and its related buildings housed three amphitheaters and city offices. Across the street were the library, museum, and, reflecting the great emphasis on physical activity, a large indoor pool or "hydro-therapy building," a gymnasium, and training track.

60.   The assembly hall. On the façade are two quotes from Emile Zola's utopian novel, Travail. Zola's novel, written at the same time as the planning of the city, was inspired by the socialist work of Charles Fourier. Like Fourier, Garnier believed that man was basically good, and so his city contained no law court, police force, jail, or church. With capitalism expelled, Garnier believed there would be no swindlers, robbers, or murderers.

61. and 62.   (facing page) In planning the residences, every room was designed so that at least one window would "allow the direct rays of the sun to enter."

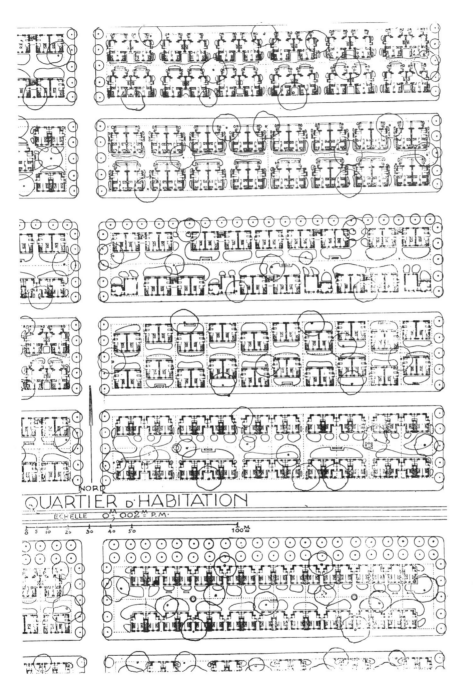

QUARTIER D'HABITATION
ECHELLE 0ᵐ002ᵐ P.M.

63.   The streets were laid out running east–west, so all the houses could face south. Tree planting was carefully controlled to allow good solar exposure. This was done more with health in mind than heating. Sun and proper ventilation were believed to cure many illnesses, including tuberculosis.

64. and 65.   (facing page) Within the grid of the city, the residences are placed in a parklike setting. No residence may take up more than half of its lot. The city was built on a two-story average.

66.   *The railroad station. The large clock tower was visible throughout the entire city.*

67.   The furnaces. The princi-
pal factory of La Cité Industrielle
is for metallurgy, consequently,
the blast furnaces. Local mines
produced the raw materials from
which the factory manufactured
iron products and machines.

THE GLORIES OF THE METROPOLIS

NEW York had all the iridescence of the beginning of the world. The returning troops marched up Fifth Avenue and girls were instinctively drawn east and north toward them—this was the greatest nation and there was gala in the air," wrote F. Scott Fitzgerald of the New York he saw on the eve of the 1920s. "There was already the tall, white city of today, already the feverish activity of the boom."

The Jazz Age city was alive with speculation—Fitzgerald's own barber had placed a winning bet and retired—and the city reached for the sky with taller and taller buildings. Sixty stories, 80 stories today, 100 stories, 250 stories tomorrow—why not? Streets in the air, apartments on bridges, airplane hangars on skyscrapers, life in the clouds, a glorious future awaited.

There was a fascination with speed and height, captured in Antonio Sant'Elia's vision of 1914, Citta Nuova, and in the shadowy cliffs of the buildings drawn by Hugh Ferriss and Raymond Hood.

68.   (facing page) The dance of the city. A scene from the dance sequence in Busby Berkeley's film, 42nd Street (1933). (Museum of Modern Art)

69.   (above) The rush of the city. Harvey Wiley Corbett's 1926 proposal to separate pedestrians from automobiles.

66437

LA CITTA NUOVA

WE no longer feel ourselves to be the men of the cathedrals and ancient moot halls, but men of the great hotels, railway stations, giant roads, colossal harbours, covered markets, glittering arcades, reconstruction areas and salutary slum clearances," wrote Antonio Sant'Elia in 1914.

Sant'Elia was part of the Italian Futurist movement that wanted to overturn the old city to make way for the new, mechanical world. The Futurists aimed to shock the public with their manifestos. "Get a hold of picks, axes, hammers and demolish, demolish without pity the venerated city," was a typical pronouncement. Sant'Elia wrote: "It is time to have done with funereal commemorative architecture . . . architecture must be something more vital than that, and we can best attain that something by blowing sky-high, for a start, all those monuments and monumental pavements, arcades, and flights of steps, by digging out our streets and piazzas."

The Futurists celebrated speed, and Sant'Elia expressed this in his designs for a Citta Nuova (1913): "We must invent and rebuild our Modern city like an immense and tumultuous shipyard, active, mobile and everywhere dynamic, and the modern building, like a gigantic machine. Lifts must no longer hide away like solitary worms in the stairwells, but the stairs—now useless—must be abolished, and the lifts must swarm up the façades like serpents of glass and iron. The house of cement, iron and glass, without carved or painted ornament, rich only in the inherent beauty of its lines and modeling, extraordinarily brutish in its mechanical simplicity, as big as need dictates, and not merely as zoning rules permit, must rise from the brink of a tumultuous abyss; the street which, itself, will no longer lie like a doormat at the level of the thresholds, but plunge stories deep into the earth, gathering up the traffic of the metropolis connected for necessary transfers to metal catwalks and high-speed conveyor belts."

Sant'Elia never worked out his ideas in detail. He was killed at the Italian front in 1916.

70.   "Lifts must swarm up the façades like serpents of glass and iron." A stepped-back block of flats, Casa a Gradinate, showing the exterior elevator tower connected by bridges to the building. On the roof is an illuminated skyline advertisement.

71.   "The modern building like a gigantic machine. . . ." Antonio Sant'Elia's 1914 project for a skyscraper. On the exterior are the elevated towers, and the building straddles several levels of traffic.

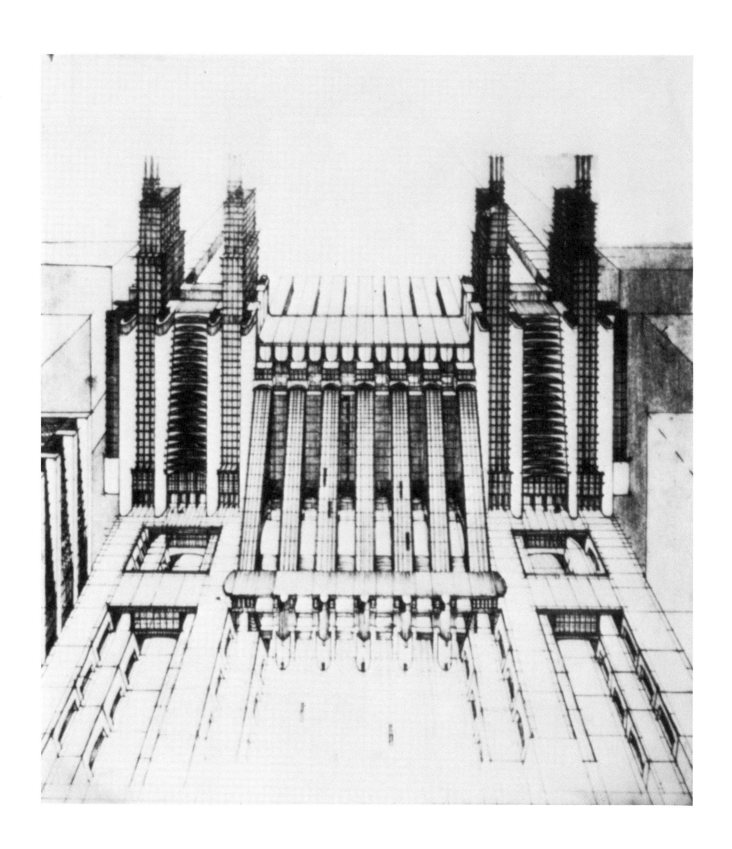

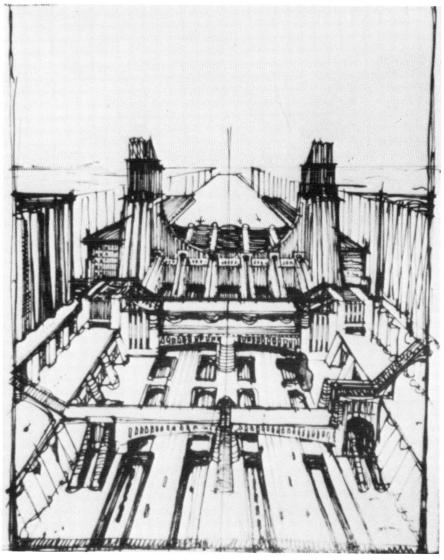

72., 73., and 74. The "Modern city like an immense and tumultuous shipyard, active, mobile, and everywhere dynamic. . . ." Two sketches for the rebuilding of the Milan Central Station. Left, a proposal for rebuilding the station that would incorporate an aircraft landing strip. Above, a sketch of a power station. In the drawings, the emphasis is on movement.

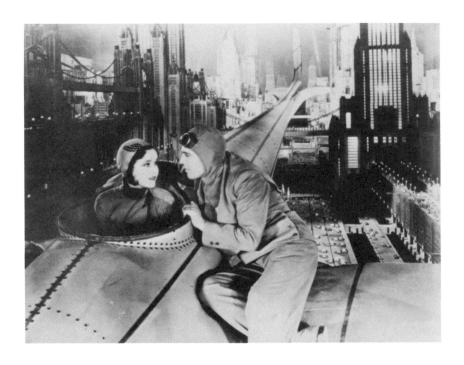

TO THE SKY

THE skyscrapers of New York tower higher, ever higher, until the mid-city has the aspect of mighty, honeycombed cliffs, deep-cleft with canyon-streets," wrote Sheldon Cheney in his 1930 book, *The New World Architecture:*

"Huge masses of steel, stone and glass are thrown skyward, signalizing the indomitable push and the irresistible lift of the creative human spirit at work. These terraced crags, these monumental up-ended pigeon-cotes, these soaring pylons and towers and piers, overwhelm us with their expression of daring, of lawlessness, of inspiration. This is at once a new Babel and a City Divine. By day it thrills us with its stupendous engineering feats, its aspiring finials, its stirring masses and directions and outlines; by night it enchants us with the loveliness of amber lights patterned on huge screens hanging from the sky, or with a tower of flame or an opalescent glow of color projected on gigantic walls."

The Depression halted the building boom that fed speculation about a skyscraper future. In 1931, the last dream building of the 1920s—the bold decade of the skyscraper future—was completed. The Empire State Building was finished in less than a year and became the world's tallest building. "There is a telescope in Madison Square Park," wrote Edmund Wilson at the building's opening, "for people to look at the tower through, just as they used to look at the moon."

75. and 76.　　　(facing page) Two lovers, "LN18" and "J21," meet in the skies over the New York City of 1980. From the 1930 musical Just Imagine. *Above, the world of 1980: skyscrapers 250 stories tall and nine levels of traffic, on the set of* Just Imagine. *(Museum of Modern Art)*

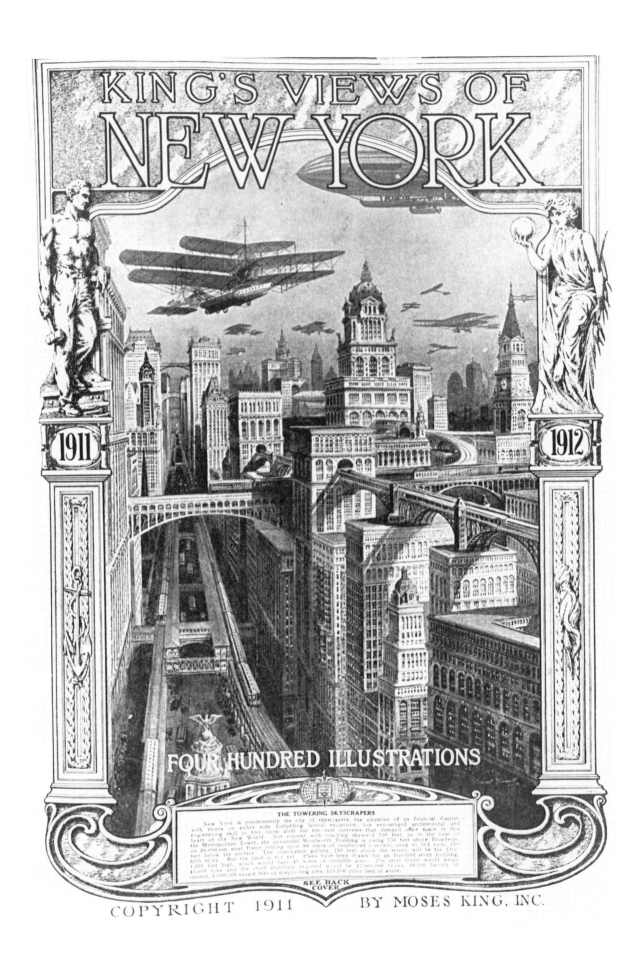

KING'S VIEWS OF NEW YORK

1911

1912

FOUR HUNDRED ILLUSTRATIONS

THE TOWERING SKYSCRAPERS

New York is preeminently the city of skyscrapers, the situation of its financial district, with rivers on either side forbidding lateral expansion, has encouraged architectural and engineering skill to find room aloft for the vast interests that demand office space in this heart of the New World. Not content with reaching skyward 700 feet, as in the case of the Metropolitan Tower, the pyramidal Woolworth Building is rising 750 feet above Broadway, its 20,000-ton steel frame resting upon 69 piers of reinforced concrete, sunk to bed rock, 110 feet below the surface. The observation gallery, 730 feet above the street, will be the fifty-fifth story. But the limit is not yet. Plans have been drawn for an hundred story building, 1,265 feet high, which would have 45 acres of rentable area. The steel frame would weigh 45,000 tons and the chief materials required would be 27,000,000 bricks, 96,000 barrels of cement, 6,000,000 square feet of fireproofing tiles, 125,000 cubic feet of stone.

SEE BACK COVER

COPYRIGHT 1911   BY MOSES KING, INC.

78. *Streets in the sky. Architect Charles Lamb's vision of the skyscraper city was published internationally when unveiled in 1908. The use of streets in the air and stepped-back skyscrapers was seen as a way toward "saving the sunshine in the city's valley of shadow," in the words of* The New York Herald.

77. *(facing page) The towering skyscrapers. "New York is preeminently the city of skyscrapers," said the caption in* King's Views of New York *(1911). "The situation of its financial district, with rivers on either side forbidding lateral expansion, has encouraged architectural and engineering skill to find room aloft for the vast interests that demand office space in this heart of the New World. Not content with reaching skyward 700 feet above the street, as in the case of the Metropolitan Tower, the pyramidal Woolworth Building is rising 750 feet above Broadway, its 20,000-ton steel frame resting upon 69 piers of reinforced concrete, sunk to bed rock, 110 feet below the surface. The observation gallery, 730 feet above the street, will be the fifty-fifth story. But the limit is not yet. Plans have been drawn for an hundred story building, 1,260 feet high, which would have 45 acres of rentable area. The steel frame would weigh 45,000 tons and the chief materials required would be 27,000,000 bricks, 96,000 barrels of cement, 6,000,000 square feet of fireproofing tiles, 135,000 cubic feet of stone."*

79.   *Apartments on bridges.
Hugh Ferriss's 1929 drawing of a
proposal by architect Raymond
Hood. "The suspension type of
bridge is assumed; the towers rise
up into fifty or sixty-story buildings; the serried structure between
is suspended—the buildings
literally hung—from cables."*

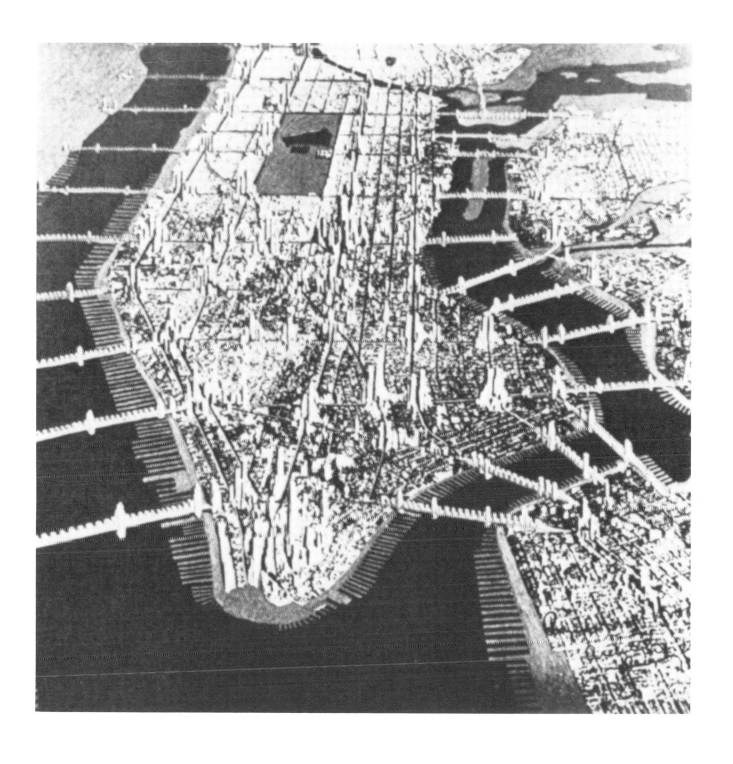

*80.   Manhattan 1950. Raymond
Hood's model shows a city ringed
by apartment–bridges (1929). Note
the groupings of the tall buildings
in the commercial centers.*

81.   The burgeoning metropolis. An aerial view of the commercial center, from Raymond Hood's Manhattan 1950.

82. *"In the future . . . the people of New York will actually live in the sky,"* said Hugh Ferriss. *"There will be aerial hangars and airplanes will be as common as flivvers."* A *"skyscraper hangar,"* circa 1930.

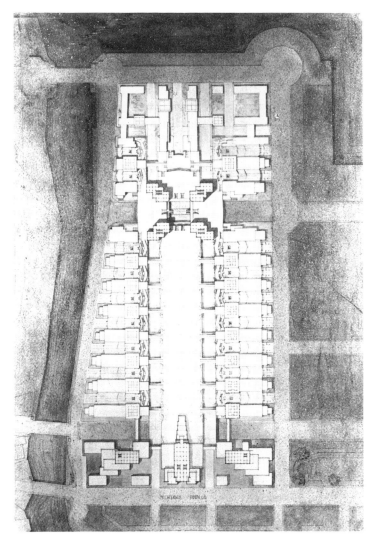

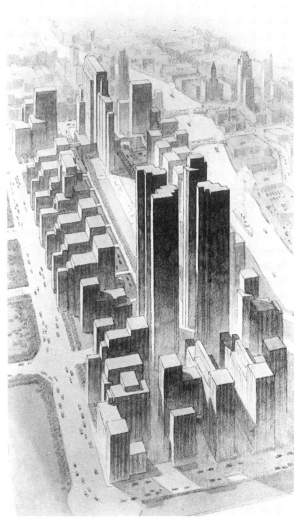

83., 84., and 85.   A skyscraper neighborhood. Terminal Park, a 1929 plan for an ensemble of skyscrapers to be built near the Chicago lakefront, prefigured the arrangement of Rockefeller Center. The plan by Raymond Hood and others was scuttled by the Depression.

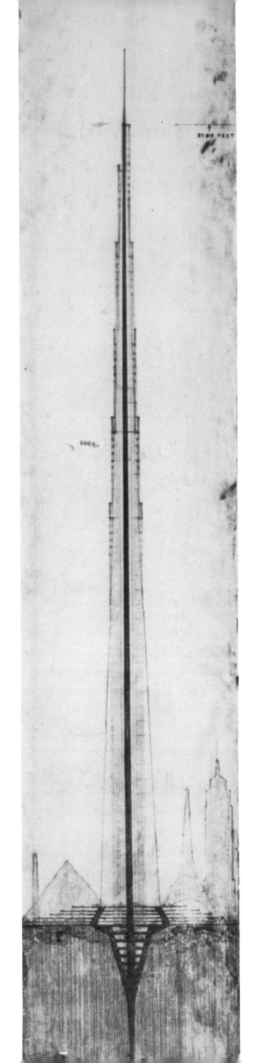

86.   Higher and higher. Frank Lloyd Wright's 1956 project for "the mile-high Illinois," rising 528 stories from its taproot foundation in bedrock.

87. *The future as nostalgia. Helmut Jahn's proposed 82-story tower for the Bank of the Southwest in Houston, Texas, would be the tallest building west of the Mississippi. In the building's design, Jahn has claimed to create a "historical continuum" by "juxtaposing the spirit and richness of past forms and present-day techniques and materials." The building's Post-Modern aspirations are clearly seen in this Hugh Ferriss-like presentation.*

TO THE SKY AND BEYOND

THE future found a home in science fiction magazines, films, and many utopian novels. The motto of *Amazing Stories,* started in 1926, promised: "Extravagant Fiction Today; Cold Fact Tomorrow." (This was printed beneath a drawing of Jules Verne rising from his tomb.)

The most popular utopian novel was Edward Bellamy's *Looking Backward* (1888). The main character falls asleep in 1887 and awakes to see the Boston of the year 2000: "At my feet lay a great city. Miles of broad streets, shaded by trees and lined with fine buildings . . . stretched in every direction. Every quarter contained large open squares filled with trees, among which statues flashed in the late afternoon sun. Public buildings of a colossal size and an architectural grandeur unparalleled in my day raised their stately piles on every side. Surely I had never seen this city nor one comparable to it before."

A flood of utopian novels followed Bellamy's, including King Camp Gillette's *The Human Drift* (1894) and his *A People's Corporation* (1924), in which young men studied "the romance of rubber." In *The Human Drift,* Gillette outlined his vision of heaven on earth, a massive cluster of skyscrapers. "Can you imagine the endless beauty of a conception like this, a city with its 36,000 buildings, each a perfectly distinct and complete design . . . surrounded by an ever-changing beauty in flowers and foliage?"

10,000 YEARS HENCE
A Prediction

88. *A city the size of New York floats several miles above the surface of the earth, "where the air is cleaner and purer and free from disease-carrying bacteria," in this illustration from the February 1922 issue of* Science and Invention. *"Gravity nullifying" devices will keep the city suspended on four gigantic electric rays. The city could be raised and lowered as needed. Benefits included constant sunlight and a lower atmospheric pressure. "Possibly, therefore, future men will have larger chests than we do."*

89.   *(facing page) Science fiction and architectural speculation run very close. This drawing of a city of the twenty-first century by Frank R. Paul ran in the winter 1928 issue of* Amazing Stories Quarterly, *but it is very close to many proposals by "serious" architects.*

90.   *City of slaves. Fritz Lang caught sight of New York's skyline in 1924 and based his future city on it in his film,* Metropolis *(1926). A vast army of workers is kept working below, out of sight, to make life seem effortless for the well-to-do above. (Museum of Modern Art)*

91.   *Razorville. King Camp Gillette was a restless inventor and an author of socialist tracts. In* The Human Drift *(1894), he sketched his utopia: a contagion of skyscraper–beehives, 40,000 towers in all, to be grouped in one "metropolis" near Niagara Falls. Most of the population of North America could be accommodated in this utopia. Each beehive was organized around a vast atrium covered with a steel-and-glass dome. Gillette soon turned his attention to other inventions and made his fortune with the safety razor.*

92.   *"Halfway to the stars. . . ." "Discopters" have replaced cable cars in this 1947 drawing of San Francisco. The flying saucers are on the roofs of buildings everywhere, and the larger flying saucers in the bay are in the cruise ship category, with shuffleboard and promenade decks.*

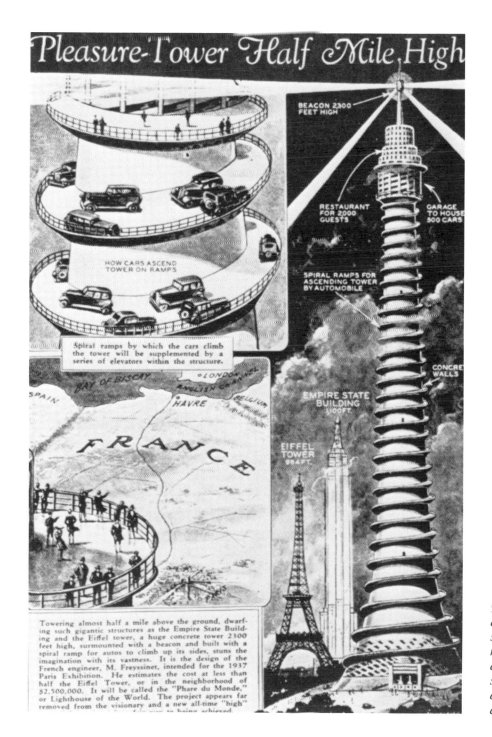

Pleasure-Tower Half Mile High

BEACON 2300
FEET HIGH

RESTAURANT
FOR 2000
GUESTS

GARAGE
TO HOUSE
500 CARS

HOW CARS ASCEND
TOWER ON RAMPS

SPIRAL RAMPS FOR
ASCENDING TOWER
BY AUTOMOBILE

Spiral ramps by which the cars climb
the tower will be supplemented by a
series of elevators within the structure.

CONCRETE
WALLS

EMPIRE STATE
BUILDING
1100 FT.

EIFFEL
TOWER
984 FT.

BAY OF BISCAY   LONDON
ENGLISH CHANNEL
SPAIN   HAVRE   BELGIUM

FRANCE

Towering almost half a mile above the ground, dwarf-
ing such gigantic structures as the Empire State Building and the Eiffel tower, a huge concrete tower 2300
feet high, surmounted with a beacon and built with a
spiral ramp for autos to climb up its sides, stuns the
imagination with its vastness. It is the design of the
French engineer, M. Freyssinet, intended for the 1937
Paris Exhibition. He estimates the cost at less than
half the Eiffel Tower, or in the neighborhood of
$2,500,000. It will be called the "Phare du Monde,"
or Lighthouse of the World. The project appears far
removed from the visionary and a new all-time "high"

*93., 94., and 95.   (here and
overleaf) A few immodest proposals from the pages of the science
magazines: tall towers, midcity
airports, and floating cities. Such
speculation sets the stage for
actual plans to receive public
acceptance.*

London to Build Mid-City Air Port

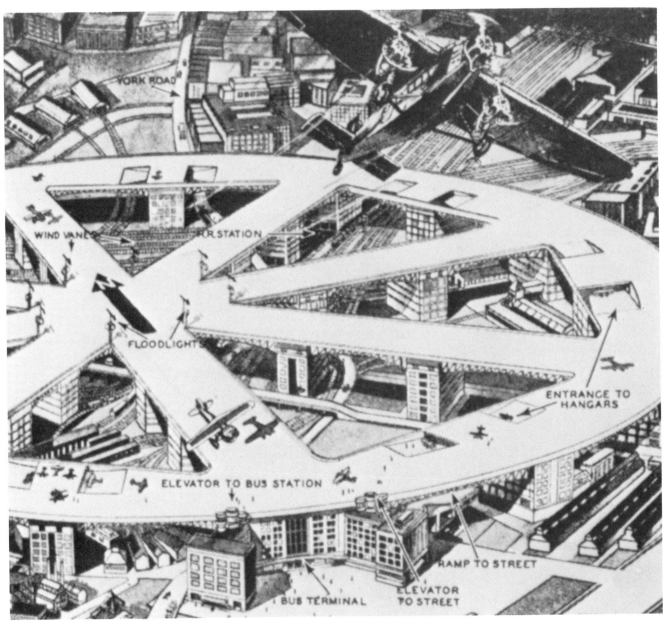

French Engineer Plans Huge Floating Mid-Ocean City

MOTOPIA

IF ever there was a marriage made in hell, it is that of the automobile and the city. They are always in the way of one another. Throughout this century, designers have tried to accommodate the city to the car. Many, like Le Corbusier and Frank Lloyd Wright, saw the automobile as liberation from the evils of the city.

A little-known inventor, Edgar Chambless, was convinced that he had the solution with Roadtown. As a patent investigator, Chambless wrote that he "began to dream of new conditions in which some of these shelved inventions might be utilized to ease the burden of life for mankind." It occurred to him to lay the skyscraper on its side, creating a continuous house and road. "I had found a workable way of coupling housing and transportation in one mechanism, and a human way for land-moving man to live—I would not cure the evils of congestion by perfecting congestion as in the case of the skyscraper—I would build my city into the country. . . . I would surround the city worker with the trees and grass and woods and meadows and the farmer with all the advantages of city life—I had invented Roadtown."

He published *Roadtown* in 1910. Chambless's idea was promoted for the next decade by *Sunset* magazine. Staying with his plan, Chambless got a hearing in Washington, D.C., during the New Deal.

Clarence Pickett served as a consultant to the Farm Security Administration and remembered the determined Chambless. "One day a tall, gaunt man came into my office in Washington, slumped into a chair before my desk, and laid a beautiful drawing on the table. His name I cannot remember, but his story was a vivid one."

Impressed by the plan, he introduced Chambless to another official. "Encouraged by our listening car, this man persisted for weeks, getting his story told to government officials and to other groups in Washington, all interested, but nobody ready to commit himself to the plan, for varying reasons. Perhaps greater frankness on the part of those of us who listened would have been a kindness; for in the end, this man could not accept the fact that nothing much was going to come of all his labors. One morning the newspapers reported that he had jumped out of the window of his hotel in New York."

96.   At home on the road.
"The Empire State Building, the
world's largest and most modern
skyscraper, and the last word in
scientific and mechanical thought,
best illustrates Roadtown," wrote
Edgar Chambless. "This giant
building furnishes everything
needed to take care of thousands
of people. Roadtown is the Empire
State Building **laid flat on its side
on the ground!**" Roadtown "pro-
poses to decentralize urban population by substituting for present
communities of congested city
blocks, new communities built in
lines, projected out through the
country and so arranged that all
business, industrial, dwelling and
other houses will be within one
continuous structure. Private
lawns, gardens and farms, thus
will lie on two sides of every
house." Chambless first proposed
Roadtown in 1910 and again in
1931.

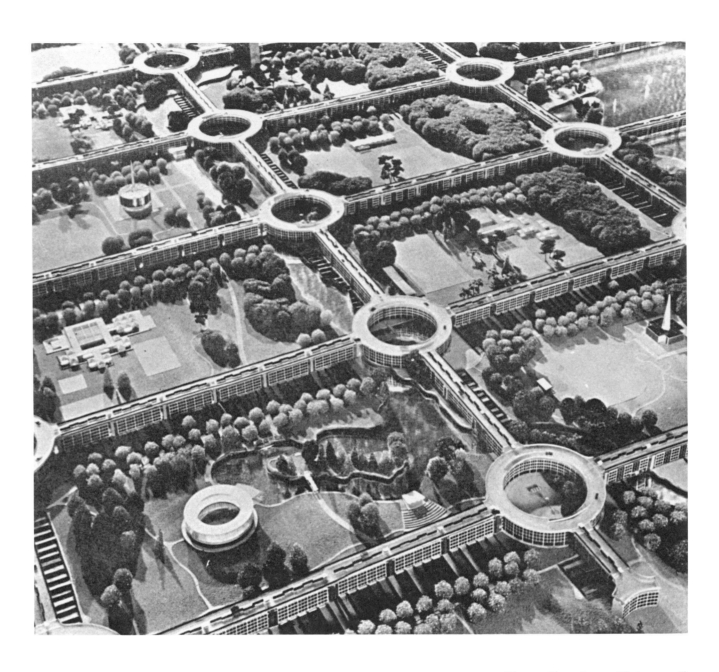

97. *Motopia, or life in a traffic circle. Traffic and parking occupy the roof, and the land in between the road/buildings is left for parks in this ideal city by G. A. Jellicoe (1961). (Praeger Publishers)*

98. *Roadtown, another view. All the building's needed services (electrical, etc.) would be in the "Endless Basement."*

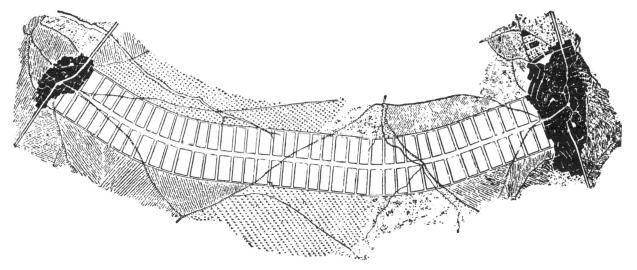

99. *The idea for a linear city has long fascinated city planners. The linear city was first proposed by Arturo Soria y Mata in 1882. This 1913 version shows a linear city linking two established towns. Soria y Mata challenged the normal concentric growth of cities with his proposal for a continuous ribbon of city that could run "from Cadiz to St. Petersburg, from Peking to Brussels." A pilot demonstration of the linear city was started in Madrid in 1894. Some 34 miles were planned, but less than half was built. The idea was taken up by an active linear city movement.*

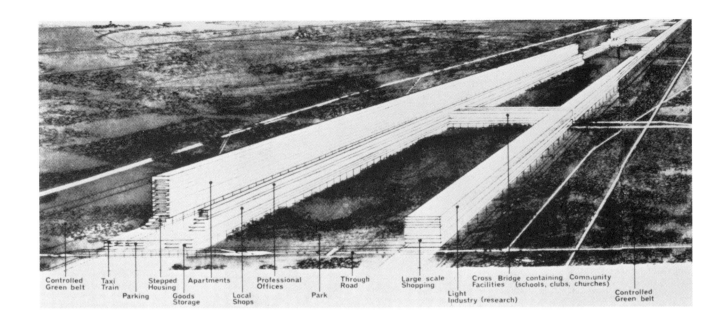

Controlled Green belt | Taxi Train | Parking | Stepped Housing | Goods Storage | Apartments | Local Shops | Professional Offices | Park | Through Road | Large scale Shopping | Light Industry (research) | Cross Bridge containing Community Facilities (schools, clubs, churches) | Controlled Green belt

100.   *"A linear city is a 20th Century city," wrote architects Michael Graves and Peter Eisenman in their proposal for the "Jersey Corridor Project," a linear city to run from New Brunswick to Trenton. They wrote:*

> *the linear city will combine the valid aspects of city and suburb*

> *it will provide for the pastoral ideal:*

>> *man in relation to nature—*
>> *his own ground*
>> *private ownership of land—*
>> *his own ground*
>> *sun, space and green—*
>> *his own ground*

The linear city, they conclude, will "prevent sprawl" and will be a "framework for a better way of life":

> *our society can send a rocket safely to the moon*

> *our society now will have a city that will send a person in dignity to the opera*

> *a glorification of our society not for posterity . . . but for now*

101.   Roadtown realized? "The American office worker would like very much to be able to drive into his or her office and operate from the automobile," architect Kevin Roche said in explaining his design of the Union Carbide headquarters in Danbury, Connecticut (Roche, Dinkeloo & Associates, 1976). The workers at Union Carbide can park within one hundred feet of their office and walk in. At the building's core are two large parking garages. Two roadways run straight through the building and hook up with ten roads coming from the north and ten from the south. With the parking tucked into the building, each office has a view out into the woods. (There are between 3,500 to 4,000 employees.) "This is an entire building uncontaminated by any kind of formal idea," said Roche. "The design grew entirely out of the initial seed of the office arrangement."

102.   "Here is the new Algiers," wrote Le Corbusier. "Instead of the leprous sore which had sullied the gulf and the slopes of the Sael, here stands architecture . . . architecture is the masterly, correct and magnificent play of shapes in the light." Highways run directly into buildings or hang in the air awaiting the building in Le Corbusier's plan for the Fort-l'Empereur section of Algiers (1931–32). "This drawing is a lesson in nature, in urban biology; it expresses the network necessary, and sufficient, for the dazzlingly efficient traffic of a city with a population of 500,000 to 600,000. It shows what must be spent on public works, bridges and roads, to achieve the conquest of Fort-l'Empereur. This is enough for 200,000 residents! Isn't it clear?"

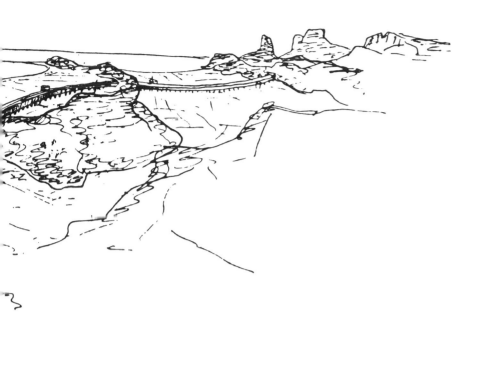

103.	The road to Rio. Le Corbusier saw a continuous road/ building as a solution to Rio's difficult terrain (1929). "You've no more land to build on? Your traffic is halted by each of those cliffs reaching down into the sea, like so many fingers on the hand of sheer, dropping mountains circling the bay? Create artificial sites, superimpose great numbers of them. Set yourselves up in the city, over the city. Glide above the city. Pillars of concrete pilotis will let you touch ground. Immediately, you give new and mighty impulse to the city. You place yourselves above the fingers that barred the way. There you are, free, 100 meters above the ground."

104.	Le Corbusier saw his road/buildings as "vertical garden cities." Here it is planned for Algiers. Some 220,000 people would be housed "royally." "The architectural aspect is stunning! The most absolute diversity within unity. Every architect will build his villa as he likes; what does it matter to the whole if a Moorish style villa flanks another in Louis XVIth or in Italian Renaissance? The uneven terrain is reached without effort, without difficulty. Footpaths wander over the very hilly ground. Cars come, on a level, along this unique and perfect highway, abundantly furnished with garages below."

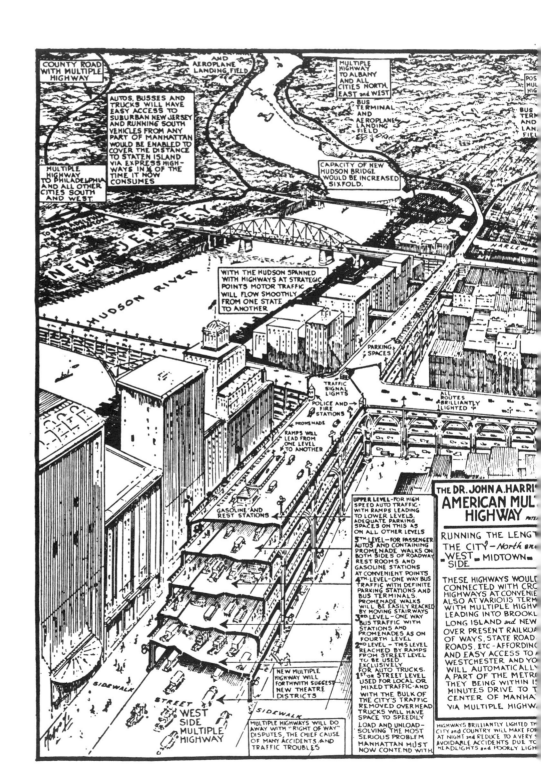

The Dr. John A. Harriss American Multiple Highway — a plan for a multi-level highway running the length of the city along the West Side of Midtown Manhattan.

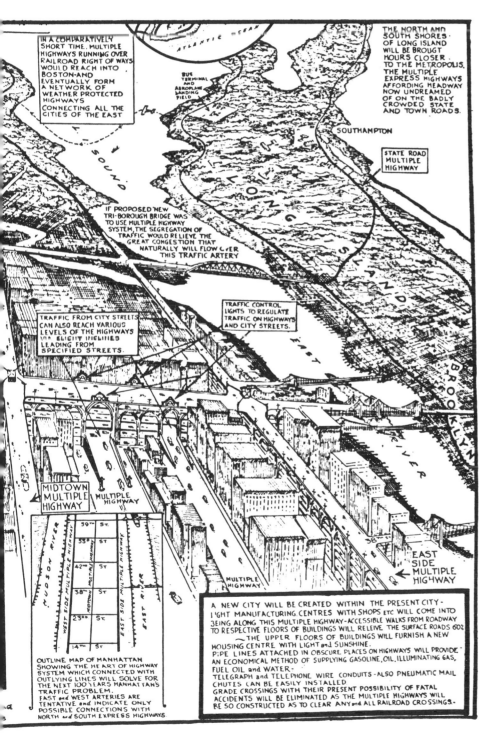

In a comparatively short time, multiple highways running over railroad right of ways would reach into Boston and eventually form a network of weather protected highways connecting all the cities of the East.

The north and south shores of Long Island will be brougt hours closer to the metropolis. The multiple express highways affording headway now undreamed of on the badly crowded state and town roads.

BUS TERMINAL AND AEROPLANE LANDING FIELD

SOUTHAMPTON

STATE ROAD MULTIPLE HIGHWAY

If proposed new Tri-Borough bridge was to use multiple highway system, the segregation of traffic would relieve the great congestion that naturally will flow over this traffic artery.

LONG ISLAND

Traffic from city streets can also reach various levels of the highways via elight incelnies leading from specified streets.

Traffic control lights to regulate traffic on highways and city streets.

EAST RIVER

BROOKLYN

MIDTOWN MULTIPLE HIGHWAY

MULTIPLE HIGHWAY

59TH ST.
55TH ST.
42ND ST.
38TH ST.
23RD ST.
14TH ST.

HUDSON RIVER · WEST SIDE MULTIPLE HIGHWAY
EAST SIDE MULTIPLE HIGHWAY · EAST RIVER

MULTIPLE HIGHWAY

EAST SIDE MULTIPLE HIGHWAY

Outline map of Manhattan showing the heart of highway system which connected with outlying lines will solve for the next 100 years Manhattan's traffic problem. East and West arteries are tentative and indicate only possible connections with North and South express highways.

A new city will be created within the present city - light manufacturing centres with shops etc will come into being along this multiple highway-accessible walks from roadway to respective floors of buildings will relieve the surface roads 60% — the upper floors of buildings will furnish a new housing centre with light and sunshine.

Pipe lines attached in obscure places on highways will provide an economical method of supplying gasoline, oil, illuminating gas, fuel oil and water -

Telegraph and telephone wire conduits - also pneumatic mail chutes can be easily installed.

Grade crossings with their present possibility of fatal accidents will be eliminated as the multiple highways will be so constructed as to clear any and all railroad crossings.

105.   A six-deck street In 1927, Dr. John A. Harriss, a former Special Deputy Police Commissioner in charge of traffic for New York City, proposed a series of three six-deck highways running north and south in Manhattan, connecting with several crosstown highways. Bridges would take the six-deck roads out of the city. Traffic on the six decks was carefully divided. The sixth, or upper level, was reserved for high-speed automobile traffic. The fifth level was for slower car traffic; the fourth and third levels for one-way bus traffic; the second for trucks; and the first, or street level, for local and mixed traffic. The decks would be built with a "flexible, or elastic pavement," and there could also be moving sidewalks. The good news: parking is allowed on all levels. "In short, a comprehensive plan providing for the solving of the traffic problem," said Harriss. And a solution for the whole country. It "may be extended at a practicable and commercial cost throughout the country so as to provide a network of **weather-protected self-ventilating highways.***"*

106. In 1950, Robert Moses, the "power broker" and head of the Port Authority, proposed a Mid-Manhattan Expressway along 30th Street. The road would be suspended about 100 feet above the street. One of Moses's supporters spoke enthusiastically about the highway, which would "go through the sixth or seventh floor of the Empire State Building." The drawing here makes it look as if the road is just a story or so above the street. The Mid-Manhattan Expressway was one of the few roads Moses did not get to build.

107. Da Vinci inverted. Five hundred years ago, Leonardo Da Vinci had proposed tunneling traffic. Somehow, in all the plans for the city of the future, traffic ended up in the air.

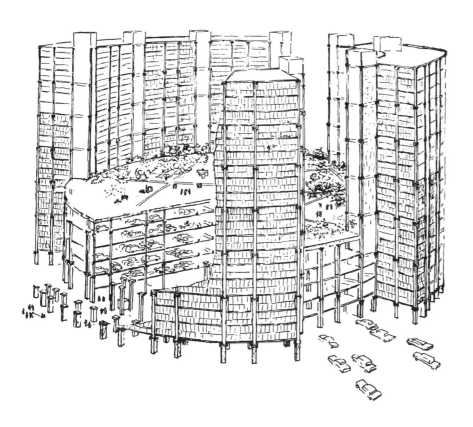

108. and 109.   Philadelphia enters the motor age. Architect Louis Kahn drew this plan for a Midtown City Forum in Philadelphia (1956–57). Traffic would feed directly into a series of circular parking garages on the perimeter. In the drawing above, at the immediate left can be seen the outline of the Philadelphia City Hall. At the far right is Independence Hall (Museum of Modern Art). The sketch at left depicts one of the stadiumlike parking garages. The outer face of the parking garage would accommodate offices and apartments (Architectural Archives, University of Pennsylvania).

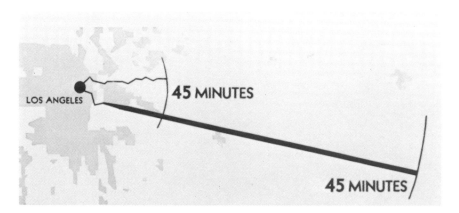

110.   A prophetic diagram. In Magic Motorways *(1940)*, Norman Bel Geddes outlined his plan for a national highway system. *''A modern highway system would extend the city's commuting radius six times,''* wrote Bel Geddes.

111.   *''The World of 1960''* as envisioned by Norman Bel Geddes and General Motors in the Futurama exhibit at the 1939 World's Fair. The future belonged to the highway.

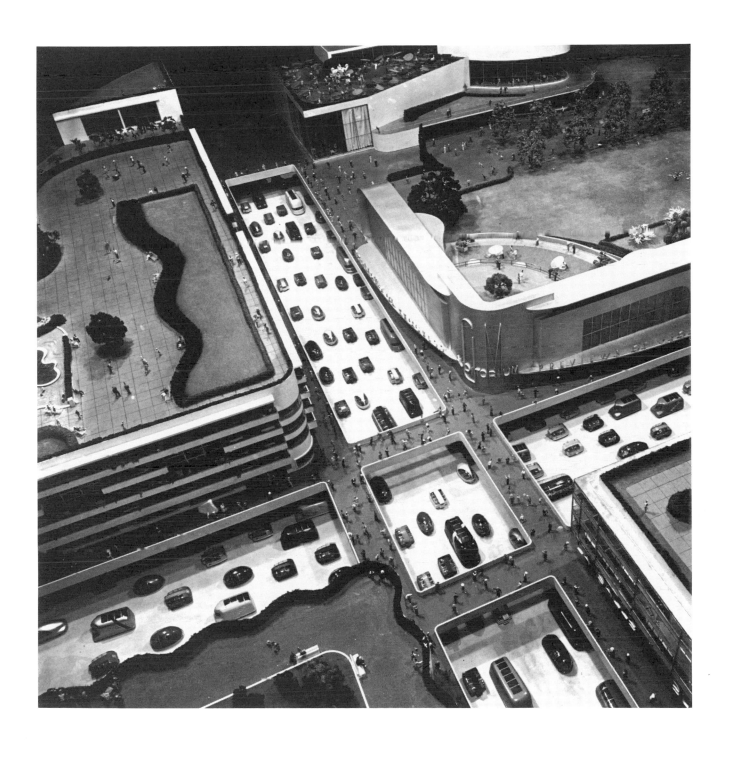

112. and 112a.   (facing page and above) The crossroads of the future. Visitors to the Futurama at the 1939 World's Fair arrived at this full-size intersection after a flight over the "World of 1960."

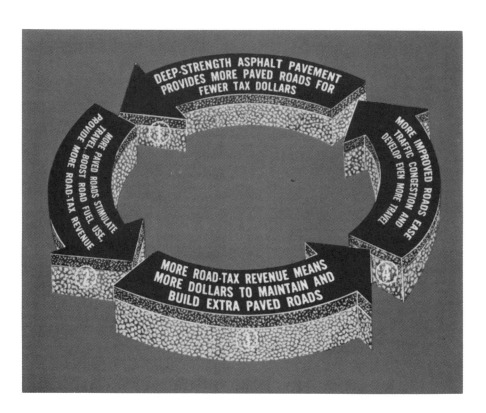

DEEP-STRENGTH ASPHALT PAVEMENT PROVIDES MORE PAVED ROADS FOR FEWER TAX DOLLARS

MORE IMPROVED ROADS EASE TRAFFIC CONGESTION AND DEVELOP EVEN MORE TRAVEL

MORE PAVED ROADS STIMULATE TRAVEL. PROVIDE MORE ROAD FUEL USE. BOOST ROAD-TAX REVENUE

MORE ROAD-TAX REVENUE MEANS MORE DOLLARS TO MAINTAIN AND BUILD EXTRA PAVED ROADS

113. The wheel of life. The cover of Asphalt, *a quarterly publication of the Asphalt Institute, April 1966. Roads beget roads.*

114. The last pedestrians fight for a place in the city, in David Keller's science fiction story, published in Amazing Stories, *February 1928.*

The REVOLT OF THE PEDESTRIANS
by David H·Keller M·D·

ALL FEMALE OCCUPANCY — APPROXIMATELY
1.5 SF/PERSON

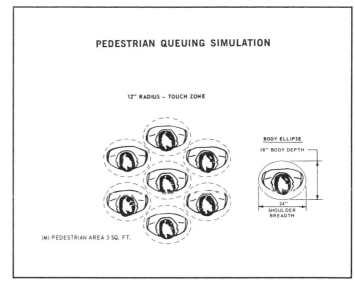

PEDESTRIAN QUEUING SIMULATION

12" RADIUS — TOUCH ZONE

BODY ELLIPSE

18" BODY DEPTH

24"
SHOULDER
BREADTH

(M) PEDESTRIAN AREA 3 SQ. FT.

115.   The crowded future.
Once out of his car, the pedestrian can expect to stand shoulder-to-shoulder with his fellow man. Above, a pedestrian queuing simulation showing the "touch zone" (a twelve inch radius around the person), and the "no touch zone" (an eighteen-inch radius) and so on, up to the twenty-one-inch radius "personal comfort zone" and the wide-open spaces of the two-foot radius "circulation zone." Other formulas carefully chart the different densities of elevator loading (all-female occupancy versus mixed occupancy) and the various ways crowds collect, exploring the "bulk process arrival of pedestrians" and the "lineal ordered queue."

The "people mover" has been the promised panacea to urban crowding. It works in Disneyland, its proponents always say. But these schemes usually entail stepping from a **moving** walkway into a moving car, creeping along at only something under two miles per hour. Alas, many people balk, the elderly have trouble, and "unused capacity will pass by."

In this version at left, people are packaged like cans and moved through something not unlike a supermarket check-out line.

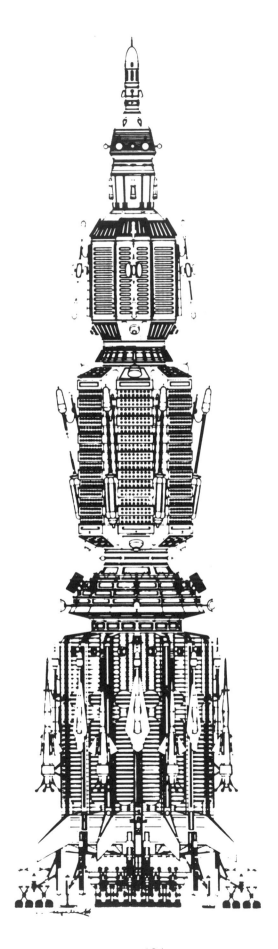

116. "Space City—Astronef 732." A proposal by François Dallegret to launch 7,000 people on a trip to Mars. An outrageous proposal, but one that was in keeping with the scale of other megastructures.

YESTERDAY'S CITY OF TOMORROW

Lewis Mumford derided Le Corbusier's Radiant City with the appellation, "Yesterday's City of Tomorrow," reducing Le Corbusier's plan to a curio.

Some of the boldest futures quickly fade to curios. In a *Life* magazine issue on the American city on December 24, 1965, "The Platform City" was strongly put forth as a possible future. In the Platform City, buildings would rise on stilts from platforms of greenery. Streets would be "tucked" underground. "The Platform City thus represents the first realistic challenge to the encroachment of the automobile on our civilization," wrote *Life,* and added that the "influential American Institute of Architects has put its stamp of approval on the Platform City as *the* essential starting point for nearly all city planning."

The article then went on to quote the president of the American Institute of Architects, Morris Ketchum: "The Platform City will give architects free reign to strive for esthetic marvels. I would think, if the leading cities of today don't keep up with this trend, they'll be just like the ghost towns of the Rockies by the year 2000. But if they do, we can build gem-like cities, surpassing any before seen on earth."

The Platform City: another proud future that has taken its place on the curio shelf, along with the many megastructures proposed in the 1960s.

117.   An aircraft carrier in a wheatfield, Hans Hollein, 1964. An adaptive reuse. For the megastructuralists of the 1960s, the aircraft carrier, a self-contained city at sea, was a form to be emulated. (Museum of Modern Art)

MEGASTRUCTURE

INSPIRED by such structures as NASA launchpads and aircraft carriers, there was a rage in the 1960s for megastructures: a one-building solution on a scale to make Daniel Burnham's dreams of wide plazas and grand vistas for Chicago look meek. The city of the future, looking like miles of inside-out plumbing and domes, would resemble an oil refinery. There were plans for twenty-mile-long cities, walking cities, plug-in cities, inflatable cities, nonstop cities, computer cities, blowout cities, instant cities (balloons and traveling cranes), and floating cities.

Reyner Banham documented the rise and fall of the mega-structuralist craze in his book, *Megastructures, Urban Futures of the Recent Past* (1976). "The most striking question left behind by all this feverish activity must always be: whence came the self-confidence, the sheer nerve, to propose works of such urban complexity and vast scale, culminating in a project by two young British architects for a 'Comprehensive City' of one billion souls stretching across the United States from sea to shining sea? The economic explanation, though handy, is too pat to be convincing," said Banham. Although 1968 was a "fat year" and "a lot of mad money was going in and out of central city redevelopment," Banham believed the explanation for this wave of giantism lay elsewhere. "Where survivors of the epoch are prepared to speak frankly, most will admit that the self competence, not to say arrogance, to propose such works came from within the profession of architecture itself; that architects had talked themselves into the position where they had no option but to propose mega-structures if they were to maintain any credibility as 'comprehensive designers.'"

118.   Walking city. Ron Herron and Brian Harvey of Archigram alarmed quite a few people in 1963 with their prankish vision of cities wandering the globe at will. Each unit contains a microenvironment and retractable sunroofs. Here, the walking cities ford the East River.

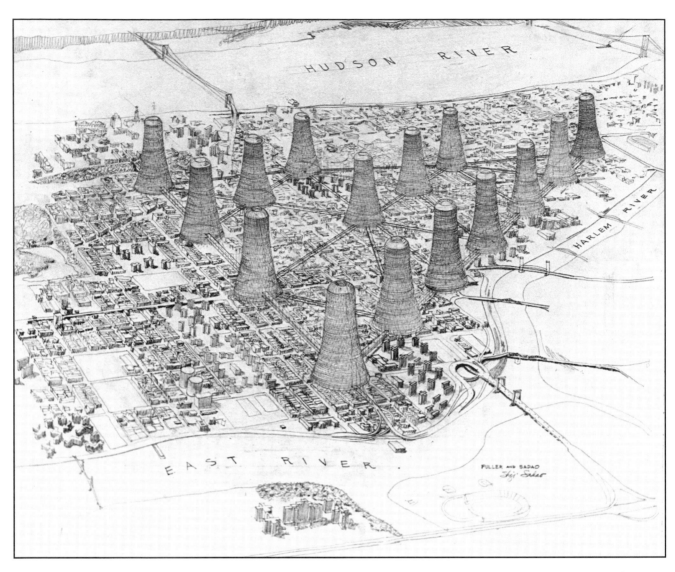

119.   Megatowers. Fifteen towers, 100 stories tall, would house 45,000 people each in this plan for Harlem by Buckminster Fuller and Shoji Sadao (1964).

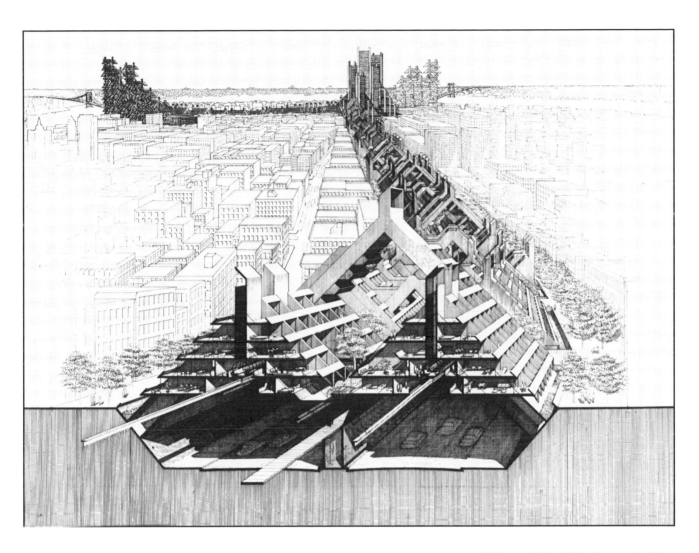

120.   Mega-Roadtown. Architect Paul Rudolph planned to cover the lower Manhattan Expressway with two sloping stacks of apartment houses (1970).

121.   (facing page) Tokyo would spread across the bay in architect Kenzo Tange's 1960 plan. A chain of parallel highway loops would start from the Imperial Palace in central Tokyo and cross Tokyo Bay to the suburbs. On the smaller branches off the loops, houses were arranged much like leaves on a tree.

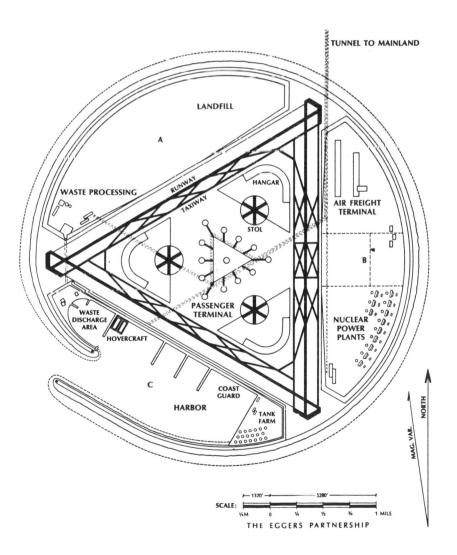

TUNNEL TO MAINLAND

LANDFILL

A

WASTE PROCESSING

RUNWAY

TAXIWAY

HANGAR

STOL

AIR FREIGHT TERMINAL

B

WASTE DISCHARGE AREA

HOVERCRAFT

PASSENGER TERMINAL

NUCLEAR POWER PLANTS

C

COAST GUARD

HARBOR

TANK FARM

MAG. VAR.

NORTH

SCALE: 1320' 5280'
¼M   0   ¼   ½   ¾   1 MILE

THE EGGERS PARTNERSHIP

122.   Nimby Island: Sytemodule (1973). Three to four miles off Long Island, the Eggers Partnership proposed building dykes to create an artificial island. The Sytemodule would have a jetport, nuclear power plant, and oil tank farm. It "will be far enough from populated districts to prevent sonic disturbance or damage caused by jet take-offs and landings, to prevent contamination from the nuclear power plant, and will allow control of oil spills from even the largest supertankers."

131

123.　　*Slung City. A new city is built in place over the existing city in Yona Friedman's 1969 proposal. The Slung City is highly flexible—units can be plugged in as needed. The Slung City would have moving sidewalks. The streets of the old city would be used for cars and trucks. Eventually, the Slung City would usurp the old city, which would survive only as a museum of urban history.*

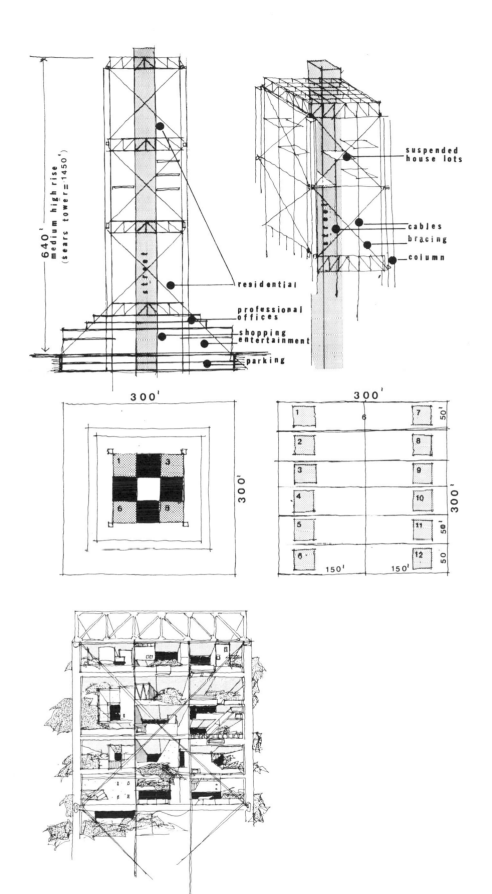

124.   The vertical suburb. Alarmed by the spread of Los Angeles, architect Harlan H. Georgesco proposed stacking up the standard suburban plot (1965–67). On land that would normally be divided into twelve tracts (300 feet by 300 feet), he proposed a vertical tract housing 200 families. On 90 acres, a normal subdivision would have 385 lots, but "the same land can be developed into five vertical villages, each containing 1,000 homes. As a result, one square mile can absorb 20,000 homes, offices, shops. . . . These villages could be constructed through the use of steel in tension. The most extraordinary example of this system is the Golden Gate Bridge. An average house (1,600 square feet) can be built on a 40 by 40-foot slab that can be easily lifted and suspended by cables at the four corners. Slabs can be spaced vertically, every 20 feet, to provide areas for two-story dwellings."

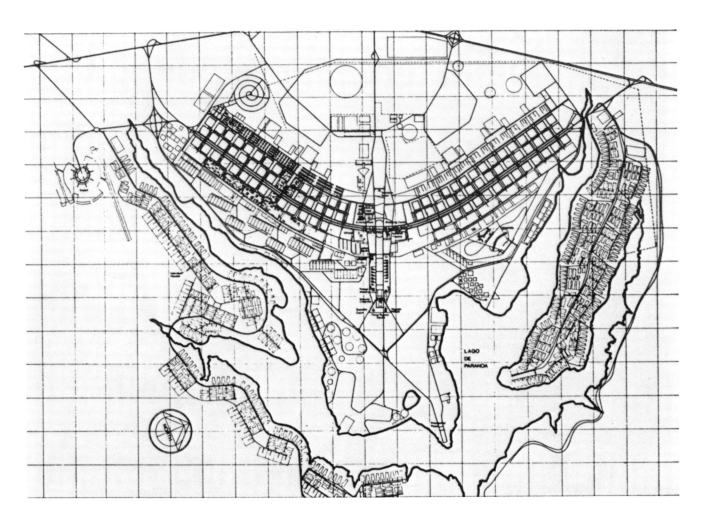

125.   While not quite a mega-
structure, Brasilia, the new capital
city of Brazil, was the talk of the
early 1960s. Above, the master
plan by Lucio Costa, 1960 version.

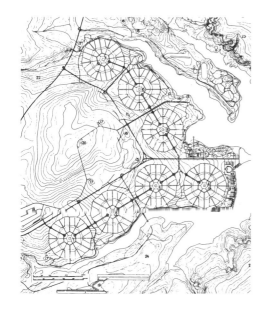

126. and 127.　　The alternate
*Roberto plan for Brasilia, which
was composed of seven circular
units of 72,000 residents each. In
this "polynuclear metropolis," no
one unit would dominate. Government
offices would be present in
each, making for a short commute.
At bottom is the "urban unit."*

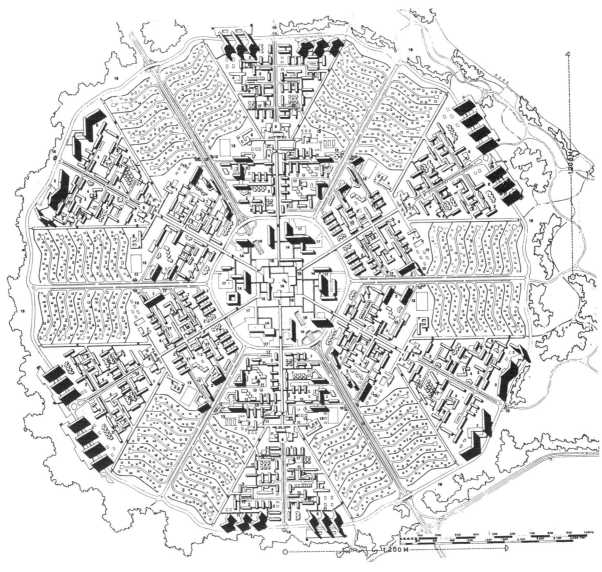

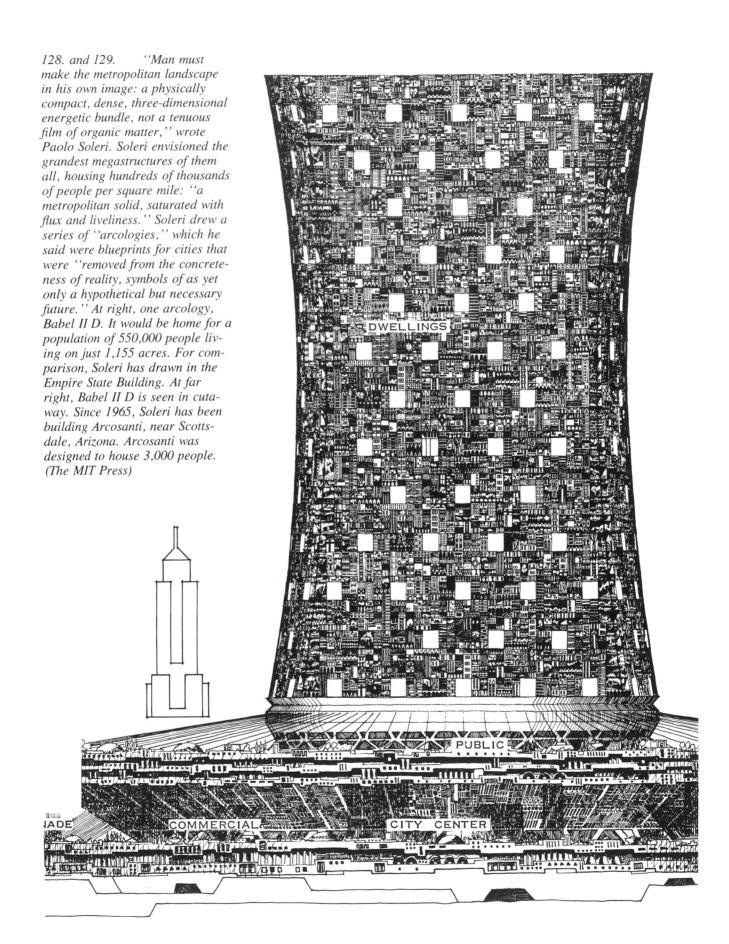

128. and 129.   "Man must make the metropolitan landscape in his own image: a physically compact, dense, three-dimensional energetic bundle, not a tenuous film of organic matter," wrote Paolo Soleri. Soleri envisioned the grandest megastructures of them all, housing hundreds of thousands of people per square mile: "a metropolitan solid, saturated with flux and liveliness." Soleri drew a series of "arcologies," which he said were blueprints for cities that were "removed from the concreteness of reality, symbols of as yet only a hypothetical but necessary future." At right, one arcology, Babel II D. It would be home for a population of 550,000 people living on just 1,155 acres. For comparison, Soleri has drawn in the Empire State Building. At far right, Babel II D is seen in cutaway. Since 1965, Soleri has been building Arcosanti, near Scottsdale, Arizona. Arcosanti was designed to house 3,000 people. (The MIT Press)

DWELLINGS

PUBLIC

NADE   COMMERCIAL   CITY CENTER

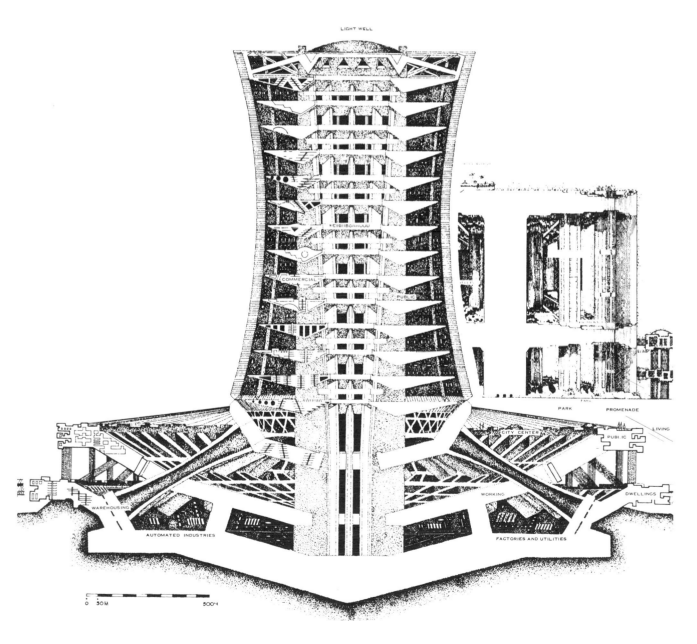

LIGHT WELL

NEIGHBORHOOD

COMMERCIAL

PUBLIC

PARK   PROMENADE

CITY CENTER

PUBLIC   LIVING

WORKING   DWELLINGS

WAREHOUSING

AUTOMATED INDUSTRIES   FACTORIES AND UTILITIES

0   50M   500'↑

137

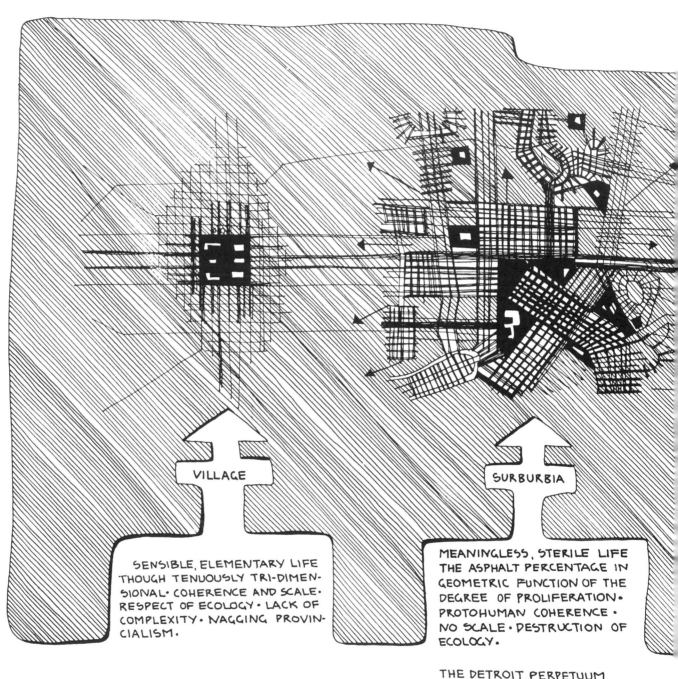

VILLAGE

SURBURBIA

SENSIBLE, ELEMENTARY LIFE
THOUGH TENUOUSLY TRI-DIMEN-
SIONAL· COHERENCE AND SCALE·
RESPECT OF ECOLOGY · LACK OF
COMPLEXITY · NAGGING PROVIN-
CIALISM.

MEANINGLESS, STERILE LIFE
THE ASPHALT PERCENTAGE IN
GEOMETRIC FUNCTION OF THE
DEGREE OF PROLIFERATION·
PROTOHUMAN COHERENCE ·
NO SCALE · DESTRUCTION OF
ECOLOGY·

THE DETROIT PERPETUUM
[AUTO]·MOBILE:
WHENEVER DISTANCE INCREASES
MORE CARS ARE NEEDED· MORE
CARS DEMAND MORE SPACE·—

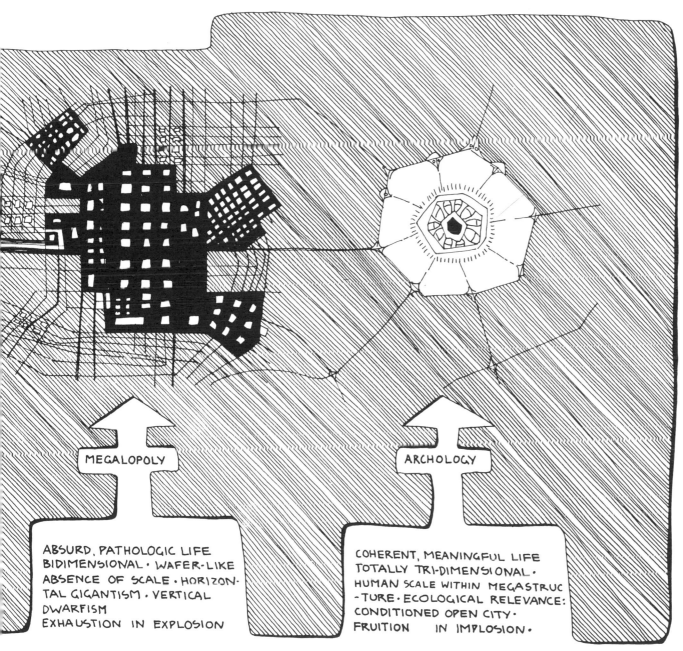

MEGALOPOLY

ARCHOLOGY

ABSURD, PATHOLOGIC LIFE
BIDIMENSIONAL · WAFER-LIKE
ABSENCE OF SCALE · HORIZON-
TAL GIGANTISM · VERTICAL
DWARFISM
EXHAUSTION IN EXPLOSION

—· THUS DISTANCES MUST INCREASE·
WHENEVER DISTANCES INCREASE
MORE CARS ARE NEEDED · MORE
CARS DEMAND MORE SPACE · THUS
DISTANCES MUST INCREASE · WHEN...

COHERENT, MEANINGFUL LIFE
TOTALLY TRI-DIMENSIONAL·
HUMAN SCALE WITHIN MEGASTRUC
-TURE · ECOLOGICAL RELEVANCE:
CONDITIONED OPEN CITY·
FRUITION   IN IMPLOSION·

*130.   The evolution of arcol-
ogy. (The MIT Press)*

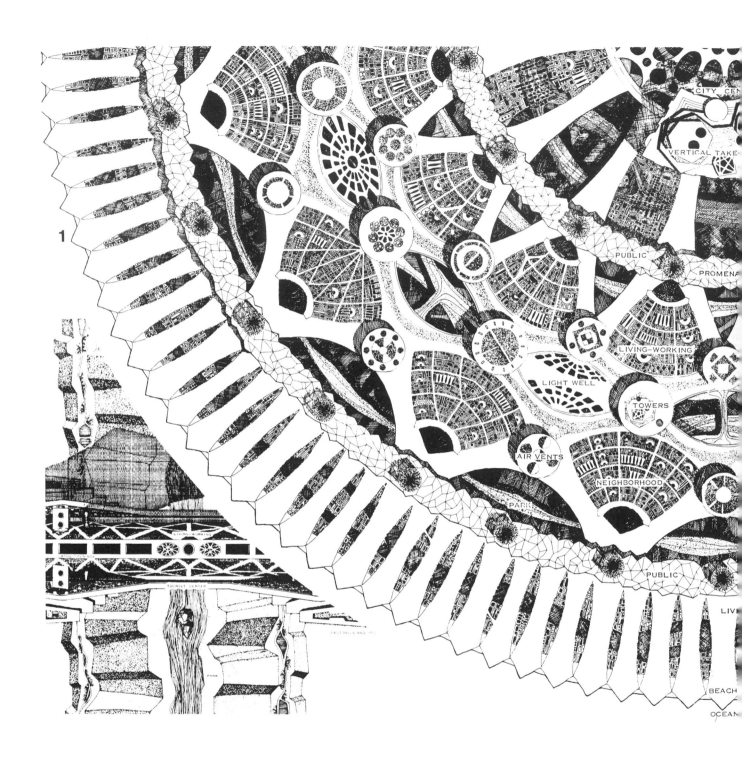

131.   Novanoah I. Looking down on a home for 400,000 people who would live on only 6,800 acres. Novanoah I would be built on the continental shelf or in the open ocean. (The MIT Press)

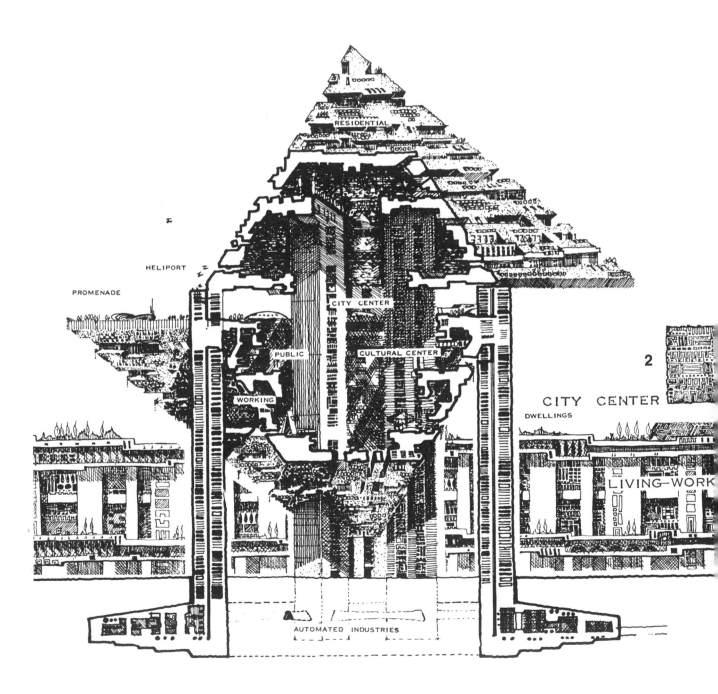

PROMENADE

HELIPORT

RESIDENTIAL

CITY CENTER

CULTURAL CENTER

PUBLIC

WORKING

CITY CENTER

DWELLINGS

LIVING-WORK

AUTOMATED INDUSTRIES

2

132.   Hexahedron. A city for 170,000 people inhabiting only 140 acres. (The MIT Press)

TOWARD TOMORROW

THERE is always the wearying prospect that tomorrow will bring the same thing—only on a larger scale. Today's city is being built on a scale not anticipated by those first critics who were warning of overdevelopment fifty years ago. Engineers have gathered to discuss the 200-story (and taller) skyscraper, and towers are rising far outside the traditional city, as suburban sprawl goes high-rise. There is, of course, a countertrend; in pockets around the country, there are architects designing "sustainable communities" and "appropriate technology."

Related to this small-scale approach is a return to the street. The much-maligned, ordinary street of stores and apartments has come back into view. The architects of this future city want to reconstruct the traditional city block and city square. The Luxembourg architects Robert and Leon Krier advocate the "restoration of precise forms of urban space as against the wasteland which is created by zoning."

While small may be beautiful, it is the big plan that gets the splashy magazine layout and the full media treatment. The gee-whiz possibilities of some new technology arriving in the nick of time like the cavalry in some old Western make for arresting reading. The small-scale solutions may have more to do with actual, day-to-day life, but we are addicted to the monster-size technological fix.

Our machines will save us, some predict, looking toward space stations; our machines will destroy us, others predict, looking toward apocalypse.

A few years ago, the Royal Institute of British Architects celebrated its 150th anniversary. They presented the drawings of top architectural students. The drawings portrayed a vision of the city after the bomb. Tribes of people farmed on the roofs of hollowed-eye ruins, grass grew in the street, and all that was once sleek now was crumbling, like a city lost in the jungle. The conviction that there is no tomorrow, no future, no utopia to fall in an idealistic swoon over may well be the most limiting factor in how our cities will look. As has been remarked, "The future isn't what it used to be."

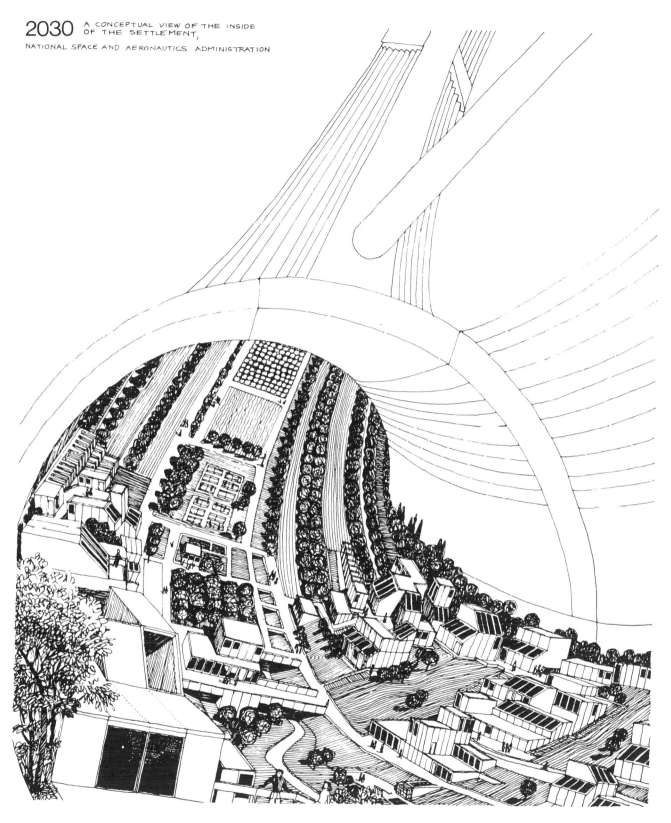

133.   The future? Life in a can? A view inside a proposed NASA space station. The possibilities of tomorrow range from life in space to. . . . (© 1981 Lester Walker, The Overlook Press)

134.   . . . Apocalypse. A photo-montage by architect Arata Isozaki showing ruined megastructures on the site of Hiroshima (1968).

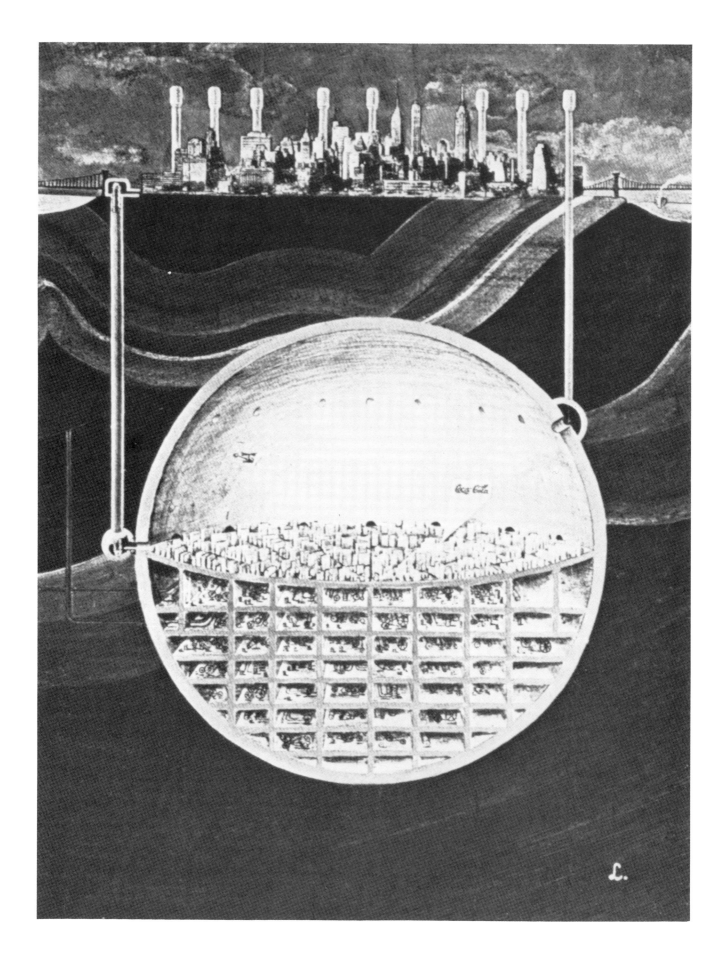

135. (facing page) Life underground. After reading that an underground atomic test had produced a perfect hollow sphere a half mile in diameter, 500 feet below the surface of the earth, architect Oscar Newman drew this "tongue in cheek" proposal in 1969. With places like Manhattan, Tokyo, and London so congested, the only place to go may be down, he said. "Manhattan could have half a dozen such atomic cities strung under the city proper, each with adequate room for manufacturing and storage in the lower hemisphere, living and working quarters above that, and full use of the overhead sphere, perhaps, for Cinerama. The real problem in an underground city would be lack of view and fresh air, but consider its easy access to the surface and the fact that, even as things are, our air should be filtered and what most of us see from our windows is somebody else's wall."

136. Civilization in ruins is a frequent theme of science fiction and modern political debate. Here's an illustration from a 1932 issue of Wonder Stories in the halcyon pre-atomic bomb era of imagined apocalypses.

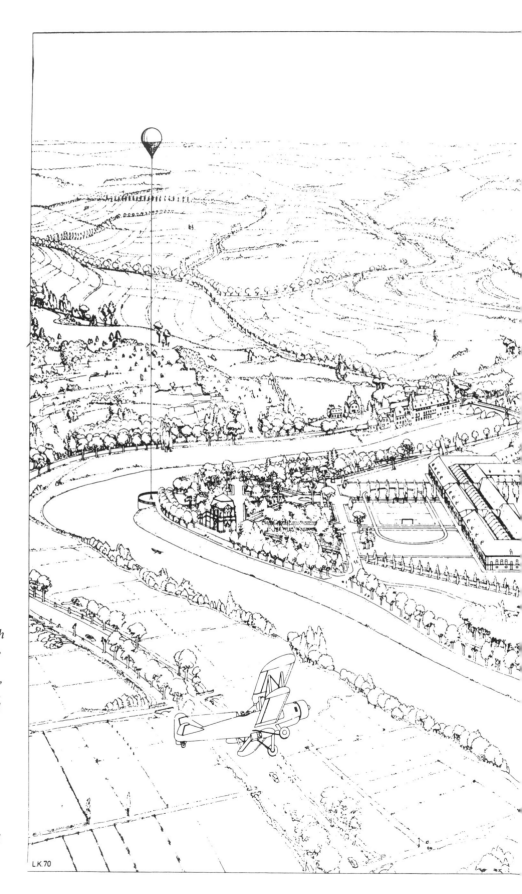

137. The return of the street. Le Corbusier promoted the "death of the street," and for sixty years, architects and planners designed towers, highways, megastructures, anything but the traditional street. With architect Robert Venturi and Co. pronouncing that "Main Street is almost all right," many future visions have come down to earth at Main Street. Here, Leon Krier's redesign for Echternach, Luxembourg (1969). Old rail yards are restructured, creating new parkland along the river. Emphasis is on carefully designed public spaces in the tradition of the old European cities.

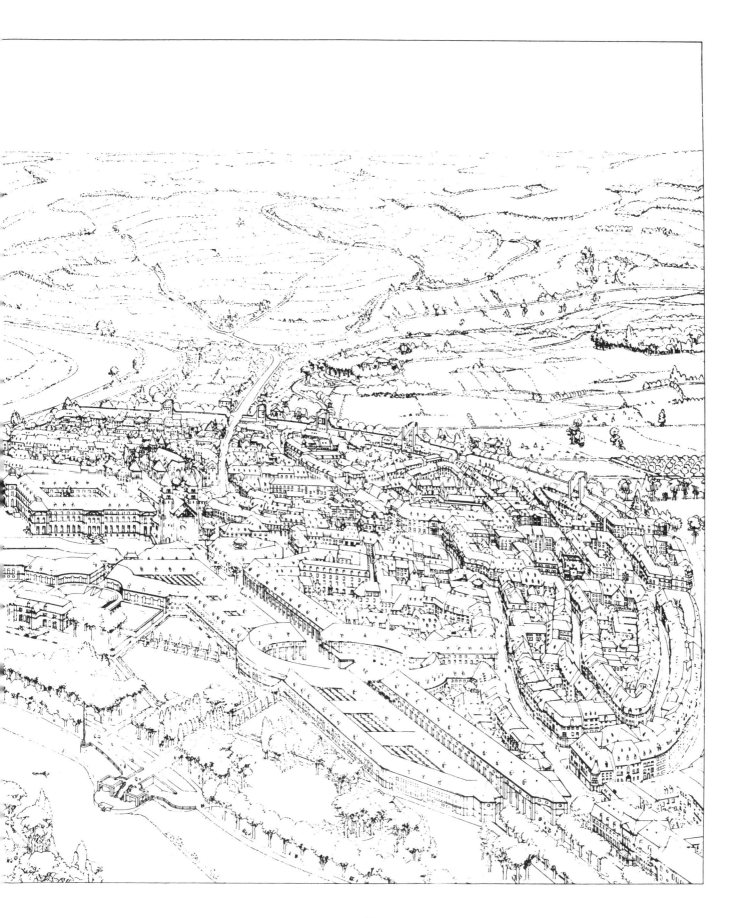

151

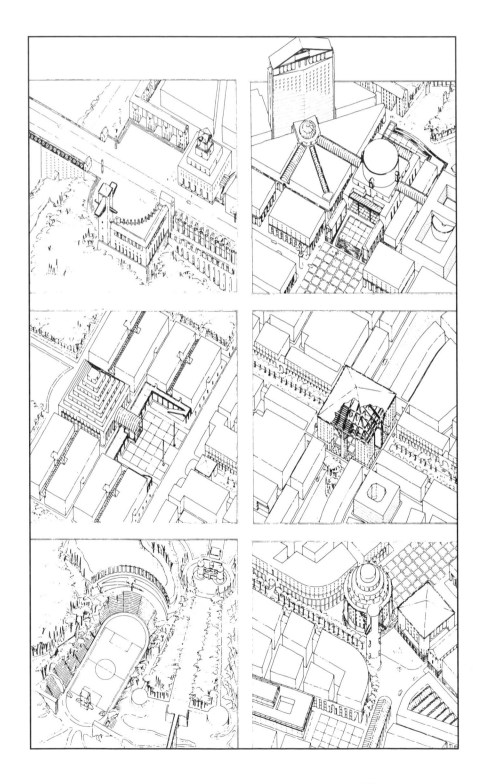

138.   Strongly defined spaces are used by Leon Krier in his proposals for reconstructing Luxembourg (1978). Rather than seeking to impose a whole new city over an old one, Krier tries to work in the context of the existing city and its history.

139.   The lost language of cities is explored in architect Rob Krier's Space Typology. His brother Leon explained that they worked for "the restoration of precise forms of urban space as against the wasteland which is created by zoning."

2

5

8

3

6

9

4

7

10

140.   A variety of urban spaces by Rob Krier.

141.   (facing page) Architects in the Modern movement tried all sorts of ways to place apartments: towers in parks, oriented to best sunlight, in cul-de-sacs. Here, Rob Krier returns the apartment building to the street. The angle of view is enticing. We are viewing the plans from a closer vantage point than the Olympian heights of earlier architects. Trees and people are in view.

154

155

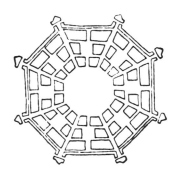 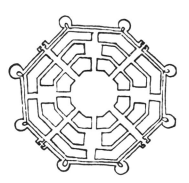 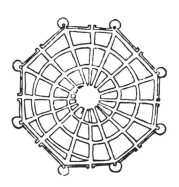

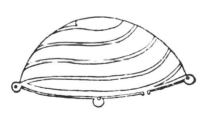
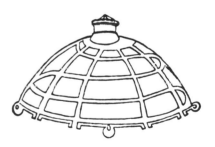

142. *Francesco di Giorgio Martini drew these studies for ideal cities hundreds of years ago. Circles, spirals, stars, grids, garden cities, tower cities have followed. The future city, and the ideal city—what is it? . . . (The MIT Press)*

SELECTED BIBLIOGRAPHY

Abercrombie, Stanley. *Architecture as Art.* New York: Harper & Row, 1986.

Ashton, Dore, and Guido Ballo. *Antonia Sant'Elia Exhibition Catalogue.* New York: Cooper Union, 1986.

Banham, Reyner. *Megastructures, Urban Futures of the Recent Past.* New York: Harper & Row, 1976.

_____ . *Theory and Design in the First Machine Age.* Cambridge: MIT Press, 1981.

Barnett, Jonathan. *The Elusive City.* New York: Harper & Row, 1986.

Bel Geddes, Norman. *Horizons.* Boston: Little, Brown, 1932.

_____ . *Magic Motorways.* New York: Random House, 1940.

Benedikt, Michael. *For an Architecture of Reality.* New York: Lumen Books, 1987.

Benevolo, Leonardo. *The History of the City.* Cambridge: MIT Press, 1980.

Blake, Peter. *Form Follows Fiasco: Why Modern Architecture Hasn't Worked.* Boston: Atlantic Monthly Press, 1977.

Bloom, Benjamin. *New York Photographs, 1850–1950.* New York: E. P. Dutton, 1982.

Boyer, Paul. *By the Bomb's Early Light.* New York: Pantheon, 1986.

Bush, Donald J. *The Streamlined Decade.* New York: George Braziller, 1975.

Caro, Robert A. *The Power Broker.* New York: Random House, 1974.

Ciucci, Giorgio, et al. *The American City, from Civil War to New Deal.* Cambridge: MIT Press, 1979.

Clarke, I. F. *The Pattern of Expectation.* New York: Basic Books, 1979.

Collins, George. *Visionary Drawings of Architecture and Planning.* Cambridge: MIT Press, 1979.

Corn, Joseph. *Imagining Tomorrow.* Cambridge: MIT Press, 1986.

Corn, Joseph, and Brian Horrigan. *Yesterday's Tomorrows.* New York: Summit Books, 1984.

Ferriss, Hugh. *The Metropolis of Tomorrow.* Princeton: Princeton Architectural Press, 1986.

Fishman, Robert. *Urban Utopias of the Twentieth Century.* New York: Basic Books, 1977.

Frampton, Kenneth. *Modern Architecture.* New York: Oxford University Press, 1980.

Fuller, Blake. *The Cliff Dwellers.* New York: Irvington, 1981.

Giurgold, Ronaldo. *Louis I. Kahn, Architect.* Boulder, Colo.: Westview Press, 1975.

Goodman, Robert. *After the Planners.* New York: Simon & Schuster, 1971.

Howard, Ebenezer. *Garden Cities of To-Morrow.* Cambridge: MIT Press, 1965.

Hughes, Robert. *The Shock of the New.* New York: Alfred A. Knopf, 1981.

Huxtable, Ada Louise. *The Tall Building Artistically Reconsidered.* New York: Pantheon, 1986.

Jacobs, Allan B. *Looking at Cities.* Cambridge: MIT Press, 1985.

Jencks, Charles, with William Chaitkin. *Architecture Today.* New York: Harry N. Abrams, 1982.

Kaufmann, Edgar, and Ben Raeburn, eds. *Frank Lloyd Wright: Writings and Buildings.* New York: Meridan Books, 1960.

Klotz, Henrich. *Post Modern Visions.* New York: Abbeville Press, 1985.

Kostoff, Spiro. *A History of Architecture.* New York: Oxford University Press, 1985.

_____ , ed. *The Architect.* New York: Oxford University Press, 1977.

Krueckeberg, Donald, ed. *Introduction to Planning History in the United States.* New Brunswick, N.J.: Center for Urban Policy Research, Rutgers University, 1983.

Kyle, David. *Pictorial History of Science Fiction.* London: Hamlyn, 1976.

Lampugnani, Vittorio Magnago, ed. *Encyclopedia of 20th-Century Architecture.* New York: Harry N. Abrams, 1986.

Le Corbusier. *The Radiant City.* New York: Orion Press, 1967.

Lynch, Kevin. *Good City Form.* Cambridge: MIT Press, 1981.

Manuel, Frank E., and Fritzie P. Manuel. *Utopian Thought in the Western World.* Cambridge: Belknap/Harvard, 1979.

Mujica, Francisco. *History of the Skyscraper.* New York: Da Capo, 1977.

Mumford, Lewis. *The Pentagon of Power.* New York: Harcourt, Brace & Jovanovich, 1970.

_____ . *The Urban Prospect.* New York: Harcourt, Brace & World, 1968.

Newton, Norman T. *Design on the Land.* Cambridge: Harvard, 1971.

Onosko, Tim. *Wasn't the Future Wonderful?* New York: E. P. Dutton, 1979.

Portoghesi, Paolo. *Post Modern.* New York: Rizzoli, 1983.

Ross, Michael Franklin. *Beyond Metabolism: The New Japanese Architecture.* New York: McGraw-Hill, 1978.

Saint, Andrew. *The Image of the Architect.* New Haven: Yale University Press, 1985.

Sky, Alison, and Michelle Stone. *Unbuilt America.* New York: McGraw-Hill, 1976.

Soleri, Paolo. *Arcology: The City in the Image of Man.* Cambridge: MIT Press, 1969.

Stern, Robert A. M. *Raymond Hood.* New York: Rizzoli, 1982.

Tafuri, Manfredo, and Francesco Dal Co. *Modern Architecture.* New York: Harry N. Abrams, 1979.

Tod, Ian, and Michael Wheeler. *Utopia: An Illustrated History.* New York: Harmony Books, 1978.

Trancik, Roger. *Finding Lost Space.* New York: Van Nostrand Reinhold, 1986.

Van der Ryn, Sim, and Peter Calthorpe. *Sustainable Communities.* San Francisco: Sierra Club Books, 1986.

Von Eckardt, Wolf. *A Place to Live.* New York: Dell Publishing, 1967.

Walden, Russell, ed. *The Open Hand: Essays on Le Corbusier.* Cambridge: MIT Press, 1977.

White, E. B. *One Man's Meat.* New York: Harper & Row, 1944.

Whyte, William H. *The Social Life of Small Urban Spaces.* Washington, D.C.: Conservation Foundation, 1980.

Wiebenson, Dora. *Tony Garnier: The Cité Industrielle.* New York: George Braziller, 1969.

Wright, Frank Lloyd. *The Living City.* New York: Mentor Books, 1958.

Wright, Gwendolyn. *Building the Dream.* New York: Pantheon Books, 1981.

CREDITS

1. The Amaryllis Press, Inc.

2. © ARS N.Y./Pollock–Krasner Foundation, 1990.

3. Reprinted from *The Metropolis of Tomorrow,* by Hugh Ferriss. Published by Princeton Architectural Press.

7. Courtesy of Da Capo Press.

8, 9, 10. Reprinted from *The Metropolis of Tomorrow,* by Hugh Ferriss. Published by Princeton Architectural Press.

11. Courtesy of General Motors Corporation.

12. Courtesy of the Cooper-Hewitt Museum, Smithsonian Institution/Art Resource, New York.

13. Courtesy of General Motors Corporation.

14. Architect. Robert Sobel/Emery Roth & Sons, P.C., New York City.

15. From Leonardo Benevolo, *The History of the City* (Cambridge, MA: The MIT Press), 1980. All rights reserved. First published in Great Britain by Scolar Press. This translation by Geoffrey Culverwell, copyright © Scolar Press, 1980. *Storia della Citta* published in Italy 1975 by Editori Laterza, Rome. Copyright © Editori Laterza, 1975. Reprinted with permission.

18. Brown Brothers, Sterling, Pennsylvania.

19. Ferdinand Janin, Chicago, Elevation Showing the Group of Buildings Constituting the Proposed Civic Center. Detail of Plate 131 in the Plan of Chicago, 1909, ink on paper, 102.9 x 305.3 cm. On permanent loan to the Art Institute of Chicago from the City of Chicago, RX17016.27. © 1990 The Art Institute of Chicago. All Rights Reserved. Plate not reproduced in its entirety.

20. Jules Guérin for D. H. Burnham and E. H. Bennett, Chicago. View Looking West of the Proposed Civic Center Plaza. Plate 132 in the Plan of Chicago, 1908, watercolor and pencil on paper, 76 x 105.5 cm. On permanent loan to the Art Institute of Chicago from the City of Chicago, RX17016.28. © 1990 The Art Institute of Chicago. All Rights Reserved.

21. Jules Guérin for D. H. Burnham and E. H. Bennett, Chicago. Plan of the Proposed Group of Municipal Buildings or Civic Center. Plate 130 in the Plan of Chicago, 1909, ink and wash on paper, 67.8 x 65.8 cm. On permanent loan to the Art Institute of Chicago from the City of Chicago, RX17016.26. © 1990 The Art Institute of Chicago. All Rights Reserved.

83, 84, 85. © Haines Lundberg Waehler, Architect. Courtesy of Haines Lundberg Waehler, successor firm to Voorhees, Gmelin & Walker.

86. Copyright © The Frank Lloyd Wright Foundation 1957.

87. Helmut Jahn. Courtesy C.F. Murphy Associates, Architects, Chicago.

90. Courtesy of The Museum of Modern Art/Film Stills Archive, New York.

92. © Alexander G. Weygers.

97. From G. A. Jellicoe, *Motopia* (New York, NY: Praeger Publishers), 1961. Reprinted with permission.

100. Michael Graves, Peter Eisenman, Architects.

101. Courtesy of Kevin Roche, John Dinkeloo and Associates, Hamden, Connecticut

102, 103, 104. © ARS N.Y./Pollock–Krasner Foundation, 1990.

105. Reprinted with permission from *American City & County,* June 1927.

106. AP/Wide World Photos.

108. Louis Kahn, *Penn Center Planning Studies,* Project 1956–57. Center City, Philadelphia, Pennsylvania. Aerial perspective. Ink on tissue, 11″x14″. Collection, The Museum of Modern Art, New York. Gift of the architect.

109. Philadelphia City Planning: Civic Center, Philadelphia, PA. Parking Dock. Louis I. Kahn Collection, Architectural Archives, University of Pennsylvania. Gift of Richard Saul Wurman.

111, 112, 112a. Courtesy of General Motors Corporation.

113. Courtesy of The Asphalt Institute.

115. J. J. Fruin, "Pedestrian Planning & Design," Elevator World, Inc., Mobile, Alabama. Reprinted by permission of the publisher.

116. Design: François Dallegret.

117. Hans Hollein, *Carrier City in Landscape.* 1964. Perspective, Photomontage: cut-out reproduction of aircraft carrier (U.S.S. Forrestal) on photograph of landscape. Mounted to board. Sheet: 8-1/2″ x 39-3/8″. Collection, The Museum of Modern Art, New York. Philip Johnson Fund.

118. Courtesy of Herron Associates, Architects, London. Design: Ron Herron.

119. Courtesy of Buckminster Fuller Institute, Los Angeles, California.

120. Paul Rudolph, Architect, New York.

121. Courtesy of Kenzo Tange Associates, Tokyo.

122. Courtesy of The Eggers Group, P.C.

123. Courtesy of Yona Friedman, Communication Center of Scientific Knowledge for Self Reliance, Paris. Illustration by Roger Hane.

126, 127. Courtesy of Mauricio Roberto, Architect, Rio de Janeiro.

128 through 132. Paolo Soleri, *Arcology: The City in the Image of Man* (Cambridge, MA: The MIT Press, 1969). Production of the graphics made possible by a grant from the Solomon R. Guggenheim Foundation. *Graphics credits:* Charles Boldrick, William Bruder, Hiroshi Hasegawa, Alan Hayward, Karen Hickey, Tullio Inglese, Rafael Jimenez Jasso, Susu Kishiyama, Jerry

Kler, Bronwyn Laird, Douglas Lee, Ursula Mandel, John McCleod, Junzo Okada, Ivan Pintar, Jacob Portnoy, Kenji Shiratori, Banks Upshaw. Reprinted with permission.

133. Copyright © 1981 by Lester Walker. From Lester Walker, *American Shelter: An Illustrated Encyclopedia of the American Home* (Woodstock, NY: The Overlook Press, 1981). Reprinted with permission.

134. Courtesy of Arata Isozaki, Architect, Tokyo.

135. Oscar Newman, Architect, for the concept and original drawing.

137, 138. By permission of Leon Krier, London.

139, 140, 141. Rob Krier: *Urban Projects 1968–1982.* Published by Rizzoli, New York.

142. Colin Rowe and Fred Koetter, *Collage City* (Cambridge, MA: The MIT Press, 1978). © 1978 by The Massachusetts Institute of Technology. Reprinted with permission.

143. Courtesy of First Garden City Heritage Museum, Letchworth, England.

WHERE SHALL I LIVE

GUIDE TO Letchworth (GARDEN CITY) AND CATALOGUE OF Urban Cottages AND Rural Homesteads EXHIBITION

PRICE 6D.. NET

Complete Plans Specification and detailed cost of over 50 designs OF MODEL COTTAGES with special articles by noted Housing Experts